THE ILLUSION OF LIFE
American Realism
as a Literary Form

FIRST EDITION, 180,000.

VOL. XXIX. JAN 15 1885 FEBRUARY, 1885. No. 4.

THE CENTURY ILLUSTRATED MONTHLY MAGAZINE

MIDWINTER·NUMBER

FEBRUARY 1885

Vedder

THE·CENTURY·CO·UNION·SQUARE·NEW·YORK
F.·WARNE·&·Cº·BEDFORD·Sᵀ·STRAND·LONDON

THE
ILLUSION
OF LIFE

American Realism
as a Literary Form

HAROLD H. KOLB, Jr.
University of Virginia

THE UNIVERSITY PRESS OF VIRGINIA
CHARLOTTESVILLE

For
EDWIN H. CADY,
who pointed out the road to realism,
and
JEAN B. KOLB,
who accompanied me on the journey

Acknowledgments

INTELLECTUAL debts begin in obscurity and end in infinity. Some, however, are more specific than others, and it is a pleasure to thank specifically Edwin Cady, Rex Cunningham, Jean Kolb, Merritt Lawlis, Peggy Marshall, Terence Martin, Walter Nugent, and Josephine Piercy. Theodore Angus, Fletcher Collins III, Michael Hoover, and R. J. Kister provided expert bibliographical assistance. The library staffs at Indiana University and the University of Virginia graciously facilitated my research, and a grant from Indiana University was most welcome.

Permission to quote from the works listed below was kindly given by the following: Hill & Wang, Inc. (*The Hoosier School-Master*); Houghton Mifflin Co. (*The Education of Henry Adams* and *The Writings of James Russell Lowell*); Little, Brown & Co. (*The Complete Poems of Emily Dickinson*, ed. Thomas H. Johnson); The Macmillan Co. (*Collected Poems of Thomas Hardy*); New York University Press (*Leaves of Grass*, Comprehensive Reader's Edition, ed. Harold W. Blodgett and Sculley Bradley); Oxford University Press (*The Prelude*, ed. Ernest De Selincourt, and *The Poems of John Donne*, ed. Herbert Grierson); Charles Scribner's Sons (*The Art of the Novel*, ed. R. P. Blackmur); Mark Schorer and Farrar, Straus and Giroux, Inc. ("Technique as Discovery"; the essay originally appeared in the *Hudson Review* and was republished by Farrar, Straus and Giroux in Mark Schorer's *The World We Imagine: Selected Essays*, 1968). Part of chapter 3 first appeared in *American Literary*

Realism, 1870–1910 (II, No. 2 [Summer 1969]) and is reprinted by permission.

The epigraph from Goethe was quoted and translated by H. H. Boyesen in his *Literary and Social Silhouettes* (New York: Harper & Bros., 1894). The illustrations from *Century Magazine* are reproduced through the courtesy of the Library of Congress. The originals of the photographs of Henry James and Mark Twain are contained in the Clifton Waller Barrett Collection of the library of the University of Virginia. The engraving of W. D. Howells was first printed in *Harper's Weekly* on 19 June 1886 and is reproduced here from a photograph loaned by David J. Nordloh, Textual Editor of the Selected Edition of W. D. Howells.

H. H. K.

CONTENTS

ILLUSTRATIONS

America, thy happy lot
Above old Europe's I exalt:
Thou hast no castle ruin hoar
No giant columns of basalt.

. . . . .

Grasp but the present that is thine,
And when thy children take to writing,
May kindly fate preserve their tales
From robbers, knights, and ghosts affrighting.

GOETHE

INTRODUCTION

AMERICAN literature has never been characterized by neatly defined periods or movements. While Cotton Mather was writing of "the Wonders of the Christian Religion" and "the Service of God" in his *Magnalia Christi Americana* (1702), Samuel Sewall was noting in his *Diary* the wonders of roast turkey, gingerbread, marmalade, apple pie, and blackberry brandy and recording his late-blooming amatory service to Madame Winthrop. Benjamin Franklin produced his famous *Way to Wealth* as a preface to *Poor Richard's Almanack* for 1758, the same year that Jonathan Edwards published *The Great Christian Doctrine of Original Sin Defended* and completed his work on *The Nature of True Virtue*. A century later there occurred that complex acceleration of American literary activity called a flowering by Van Wyck Brooks, a renaissance by F. O. Matthiessen, and romanticism by the textbooks. The unity and cohesiveness of this period are too often exaggerated, and a "romantic movement" composed of such disparate men as Cooper, Hawthorne, Poe, Emerson, Melville, and Whitman moves beyond the boundaries of precise definition. In the next generation—that of the men born in the 1830's and 1840's who came to intellectual maturity in the 1880's—the characteristically American diversity is again evident. A reader in the mid-1880's could choose from the works of Henry James, George W. Peck, Mark Twain, James Whitcomb Riley, W. D. Howells, Lew Wallace, Helen Hunt Jackson, Henry Adams, and Joel Chandler Harris. The fireside gentility of Longfellow's last works contended, incongruously, with the dime novels of J. R. Coryell and Edward L. Wheeler—creators, respectively, of Nick Carter and Deadwood Dick.

Nevertheless, in the decade of the eighties, especially around 1885, the major authors of the day—James, Mark Twain, and Howells—found themselves writing works which had important similarities in content and technique stemming from shared concepts about the art of fiction.[1] The many differences in their books cannot be ignored—Huckleberry Finn and Hyacinth Robinson would have made strange raftfellows—but the variety of these works and the obvious differences in the authors' personalities (one has only to compare Mark Twain's flamboyant steamboat-Gothic mansion in Hartford with James' old and mellow Georgian residence in Sussex) tend to make the common elements even more striking. This convergence of major talent produced an important body of writing which forms the core of American realism.[2] These works and realism itself provided the fuel for innumerable debates—"war," as Howells called

[1] The significance of 1885 for American realism was suggested by Bernard De Voto in *Mark Twain at Work* (Cambridge, Mass.: Harvard University Press, 1942, p. 102) and elaborated by Edwin H. Cady in his Introduction to *The Rise of Silas Lapham* (Boston: Houghton Mifflin, 1957, p. v): "About the year 1885 American literature seemed to strike a peak of accomplishment different from any known before and higher than any since the marvelous years around 1850. . . . At that moment . . . they [Howells, Mark Twain, and James] stood together, without on the whole having intended it, as the inventors of a new but permanent contribution to the world of letters, the American realistic novel." Robert Falk supports this opinion in "The Search for Reality": "Beginning around 1880 . . . Howells, James, and Mark Twain were in their prime and ready to write some of their finest books. . . . Among three such different talents there existed a compatibility and a harmony which in itself almost characterized the essence of American realism in the late Victorian period" (*The Gilded Age: A Reappraisal*, ed. H. Wayne Morgan [Syracuse: Syracuse University Press, 1963], pp. 211, 220).

[2] Six major novels were produced in the mid-1880's—James: *The Bostonians* (1885–86), *The Princess Casamassima* (1885–86); Mark Twain: *Adventures of Huckleberry Finn* (1885); Howells: *The Rise of*

it—in the late nineteenth century. In more recent times there has been much postwar confusion about the aims of that conflict, and even about its outcome. Realism has been variously defined and maligned. It has been sharpened and aimed backward chronologically by those who are searching for a weapon to use against romanticism. It has been expanded to embrace the naturalists and then exploded to include most twentieth-century writing.

This study will attempt to restore literary and historical meaning to the term by focusing on the period of its maturity in American literature through an examination of what James, Mark Twain, and Howells attempted and what they achieved in the mid-1880's. It will argue that style is an important and integral part of American realism, and that the three authors developed new techniques in fiction which constitute a coherent and definable realistic style. The achievements of the realists are not solely stylistic, but they are importantly stylistic, and since this aspect has been most neglected in critical writing it will be given primary emphasis in this investigation. Finally, having examined and defined the realistic movement of the mid-1880's, this study will attempt to place realism within the larger context of American literary history by showing its double-sided relationship to the earlier romantic movement and the distinctions between realism and its wayward offspring, naturalism.

Silas Lapham (1884–85), *Indian Summer* (1885–86), *The Minister's Charge* (1886). See Bibliography, pp. 147–152 below, for a summary of works produced by James, Mark Twain, and Howells from 1884 to 1886.

THE HISTORICAL CONTEXT

CHAPTER I

1885

THE year 1885 opened with a burst of the boisterous naïveté which characterized much of late nineteenth-century America. The New York *Times* for January 1 reported that turbulent crowds "blocked the sidewalks, straggled through the streets, and struggled and pushed each other . . . while the noise they sent up almost drowned the welcome to the New Year which rang out from the Trinity tower." The events of the year, sandwiched between the scurrilous election campaign of 1884 and the Haymarket Riot of 1886, seemed to justify the New Year's greeting.

On March 4, 1885, the crowds again turned out, this time in Washington—with brass bands, fireworks, whistles, streamers, and endless companies of marching militiamen—for the exuberant presidential inauguration. Single rooms rented for eight dollars a day as 200,000 spectators packed the extra coaches and special trains which converged upon the capital. "Everybody shouted as loud and as long as he knew how, and nobody paid the slightest attention to him. People lost their money, their tickets, and their companions."[1] The *Times,* reflecting the complexities and the dualities of the Gilded Age, simultaneously condemned the "wildest and strangest confusion" accompanying the ceremonies and boasted that the inauguration was conducted "on a larger scale than any previous similar occasion." At

[1] New York *Times*, 3 March 1885, p. 5. The following quotations concerning Cleveland's inauguration are from *Times* articles on 3 March, pp. 1, 5, and 5 March, p. 1.

one o'clock on March 4, on a platform constructed at the east front of the Capitol, Grover Cleveland took the presidential oath ("screams and yells and cheers rent the air as the crowds fell back in masses") and became the chief executive of a country of fifty-six million people, a country which was expanding rapidly—by almost thirteen million in the decade of the eighties—and changing in character. In 1885 nearly one-third of the population lived in cities, and the percentage was rising steadily. Approximately 3,500,000 people moved west in the year, and 395,000 immigrants, increasingly drawn from central and eastern Europe, entered the thirty-eight united states of America, many of them passing through New York harbor where a gigantic copper statue executed in Paris by Frédéric Bartholdi was being assembled on Bedloe's Island.

In the western Indian Territory there were flare-ups with the Cheyennes and the Arapahoes. Further south, General George Crook was closing the ring on Geronimo and his Apache warriors, the last act in the intermittent drama of Indian conflict which Helen Hunt Jackson, in 1881, had accurately labeled "A Century of Dishonor." In Chicago, Henry H. Richardson built the Glessner house and Marshall Field's, and William Le Baron Jenney's ten-story steel-skeleton Home Insurance Building fathered the concept of the skyscraper. The year 1885 also saw the manufacture of the Mergenthaler linotype machine, the dedication of the Washington Monument (thirty-seven years after the cornerstone had been laid), and the funeral of Ulysses S. Grant, whose immense catafalque, preceded by forty thousand soldiers and followed by hundreds of carriages, was drawn by twenty-four black horses to the tomb in Riverside Park.[2]

The publishing world also participated in, and contributed

[2] *Ibid.*, 9 August 1885, p. 1. Other factual material in this and the preceding paragraph is drawn from Richard B. Morris, *Encyclopedia of American History*, updated and rev. (New York: Harper & Row, 1965), and U.S. Bureau of the Census, *Historical Statistics of the United States, Colonial Times to 1957* (Washington, D.C., 1960).

to, what Mark Twain called "the drive and push and rush and struggle of the raging, tearing, booming nineteenth century."[3] In 1885 there were some 3,300 magazines, almost a 500 per cent increase since the end of the Civil War. Recently founded enterprises included the Kansas City *Star*, the New York *Evening Post*, the New York *Morning Journal*, Lovell's Popular Library, the *Ladies' Home Journal*, and Samuel S. McClure's Newspaper Syndicate. The New York *World*, stimulated by the innovations of Joseph Pulitzer, was undergoing a phenomenal growth spurt, climbing from a circulation of 20,000 in 1883 to 250,000 in 1886. In the fall of 1885 twenty presses and seven binderies under the direction of Mark Twain's publishing house labored over one of the year's best sellers, the *Personal Memoirs of U. S. Grant*. The two volumes of the *Memoirs* were dictated at first, and then, when cancer of the throat made speech impossible, they were written by the dying and impoverished general in his last pain-filled, drug-filled months. Grant finished the job in the middle of July and died before the month was out, but the *Memoirs* went on to make publishing history by selling over three hundred thousand sets in thirty months. It ultimately earned author's royalties of more than $440,000—a final, posthumous victory that handsomely liquidated the debts which the courageous but credulous ex-president had left to his family.[4]

[3] *Mark Twain's Speeches* (New York: Harper & Bros., 1923), p. 145.

[4] Frank Luther Mott, *Golden Multitudes: The Story of Best Sellers in the United States* (New York: Macmillan Co., 1947), p. 157. See also Mark Twain's discussion of Grant's *Memoirs* in Twain's *Autobiography*, ed. Charles Neider (New York: Harper & Row, 1959), pp. 258–263, 268–277. For a description of the late nineteenth-century publishing world, see Mott's *History of American Magazines*, 5 vols. (New York: D. Appleton & Co., and Cambridge, Mass.: Harvard University Press, 1930–1969), and his *American Journalism: A History of Newspapers . . . 1690 to 1950*, 3d ed. (New York: Macmillan Co., 1962). The *World*'s circulation figures, quoted above, are taken from *American Journalism*, p. 435; magazine total figures are from *A History of American Magazines*, III, 5.

In Boston the *Atlantic Monthly* was holding forth as usual, conservatively edited by Thomas Bailey Aldrich. The *Atlantic's* subscription rate had declined, however, and the magazine and its city were being strongly challenged from New York by *Harper's Monthly*, *The Nation*, *The North American Review* (which had made the symbolic move from Boston to New York in 1878), and the *Century Illustrated Monthly Magazine*, edited by Richard W. Gilder, a refurbished, independently published continuation of *Scribner's Monthly*. It is the *Century*, then riding the circulation crest of the first of the periodic waves of interest in the Civil War, which provides the best key to the literary achievements of 1885.[5]

In a single issue, that of February, 1885, an extraordinary cluster of major works by Howells, James, and Mark Twain appeared: a chapter of *Adventures of Huckleberry Finn* entitled "Royalty on the Mississippi";[6] the fourth installment

[5] The spectacularly successful Civil War series, Battles and Leaders of the Civil War, produced an immediate boost in circulation from 127,000 to 225,000 and ultimately earned more than a million dollars. L. Frank Tooker noted that "there were times when the normally quiet editorial rooms were like the headquarters of an army on the eve of a great battle, with generals and privates, confederates and federals, coming and going" (*The Joys and Tribulations of an Editor* [New York: Century Co., 1924], p. 46). The series was so successful that the editors found it necessary to "recommend special attention to the other contents of the magazine—to the fiction, the travel, the domestic papers, the public discussion, the art, the humor—for the most part drawn from American life" (editorial in "Topics of the Time," *Century Magazine*, XXIX [March 1885], 788). The story of the *Century* is told by its two well-known editors, each of whom spent forty years with the magazine. See *Letters of Richard Watson Gilder*, ed. Rosamond Gilder (Boston: Houghton Mifflin Co., 1916), and Robert Underwood Johnson, *Remembered Yesterdays* (Boston: Little, Brown & Co., 1923). See also Mott's excellent chapter on the sixty-year history of *Scribner's Monthly—Century Magazine* in his *History of American Magazines*, III, 457–480.

[6] The irrelevance of the charges of verbal and intellectual emasculation of Mark Twain's manuscripts that have been recurrently brought

of *The Rise of Silas Lapham*, which continued until August; the first installment of *The Bostonians*, which ran until February, 1886; and a travel sketch of Italy by Howells entitled "A Florentine Mosaic." In addition to the continuing serializations of *Silas Lapham* and *The Bostonians*, other issues during the year presented more *Huckleberry Finn*, Twain's "Private History of a Campaign That Failed," and five more travel sketches by Howells. Previously, in the summer and fall issues of 1884, the *Century* had offered two tales by James ("Lady Barberina" and "A New England Winter"), book reviews by Howells as well as the first chapters of *Silas Lapham*, and "An Adventure of Huckleberry Finn: With an Account of the Famous Grangerford-Shepherdson Feud." When *The Bostonians* ran out in February, 1886, the *Century* began to serialize Howells' *The Minister's Charge*, which continued for the remainder of the year. The three authors thus dominated the magazine from the spring of 1884 to the winter of 1886. To the thirty-one numbers issued in this period, James, Mark Twain, and Howells contributed a total of 688 pages, a remarkable 48 per cent of the fictional material.[7]

---

against Howells, Olivia Clemens, and Twain himself can be seen in the historical perspective provided by editor Gilder's omissions and emendations, which made what he smugly called a "most decided difference" in the *Century* version (*Letters of R. W. Gilder*, p. 399). See also Bernard De Voto, *Mark Twain's America* (Boston: Little, Brown & Co., 1932), pp. 212–216; Arthur L. Scott, "The *Century Magazine* Edits *Huckleberry Finn*, 1884–1885," *American Literature*, XXVII (November 1955), 356–362; and Sydney J. Krause, "Olivia Clemens's 'Editing' Reviewed," *American Literature*, XXXIX (November 1967), 325–351.

[7] In 1885 James, Howells, and Mark Twain wrote an astonishing 67 per cent of the fiction in the *Century Magazine*. Many of the other contributors to the magazine in this period also showed realistic tendencies, especially such local colorists as Edward Eggleston, Joel Chandler Harris, Mary Hallock Foote, George Washington Cable, and Mary N. Murfree.

And the *Century Magazine* tells only a part of the story of 1885, for its pages, receptive as they were, simply were not numerous enough to encompass the prolific writings of the realists in the period. The *Century* was still publishing *The Rise of Silas Lapham* in July, 1885, when *Harper's Monthly* began to serialize *Indian Summer*, which ran until February, 1886. Similarly, in September, 1885, when the *Century* was occupied with *The Bostonians*, James turned to the *Atlantic Monthly* for the fourteen-issue serialization of *The Princess Casamassima*. Having flooded the leading magazines with novels, the realists saw their shorter writings spill over into *Harper's Weekly, St. Nicholas*, the *English Illustrated Magazine*, the New York *Sun*, the *Pall Mall Gazette*, and *Longman's Magazine*. The year 1885 is thus a remarkable moment in American literature, an *annus mirabilis* for realistic fiction, dominated by the individual *anni mirabiles* of James, Howells, and Mark Twain.

AMERICAN LITERARY REALISM

An Approach to Definition

CHAPTER II

THE PROBLEM OF DEFINITION

THE works produced by James, Mark Twain, and Howells in the mid-1880's, together with certain of their other writings in the period from 1865 to 1900 and those of such writers as De Forest, Eggleston, Howe, Murfree, and Garland, have long been considered part of a "realistic" school of fiction. The term "realism" has had a remarkable vogue, although its popularity seems to be inversely proportional to the precision with which it has been used. It is a term which is in great need of clear definition, not only because of its constant general and critical use, but also because of the importance to literary study of the concepts which the term implies. It is a term which we apparently cannot do without—whether we are casual moviegoers or professors of literature. Admittedly, the definition of literary terms is often a hazardous affair, and this study will attempt to steer between the monster of hyperprecision (in which realism becomes equated with a single author or book) and the whirlpool of generality (which swallows, as vaguely "realistic" in one way or another, most of the literature of the past one hundred years). It will also attempt to avoid the related fallacies of reification, in which the defined term takes on a life of its own, apart from the literature which nourishes it, and deification, in which definition becomes an altar for the sacrifice of individual works. It is hoped that the definition of realism presented in these pages will be continuously relevant to the literature it seeks to explain, will enlarge rather than constrict, and will provide a means of seeing realistic works more clearly and placing them in meaningful relation to other kinds of writing. That, at least, is the goal.

One way to approach the problem of defining realism is to attempt to clear away the obstacles which have, in the past, hindered the process of definition. The first step is to define what is being defined. Realism is a pluralistic term—there are many realisms—and some discussions have floundered because of a failure to consider carefully the scope of the definition.[1] A definition of realism which distinguishes between Homer and the Elohist, between Chaucer and John Gower, or between Falstaff and the medieval Vice tradition, may not be useful in a consideration of nineteenth-century American literature. Ian Watt has shown, impressively, how the "formal realism" of the novel separates Defoe, Richardson, and Fielding from the earlier conventions of prose fiction,[2] but his definition is not very helpful—and it was not meant to be—in differentiating among the writings of Hawthorne, James, and Dreiser, all of whom presumably wrote novels. Thus this discussion will concentrate on the description and definition of only one kind of realism, that which was practiced most significantly by three Americans—James, Twain, and Howells—in the mid-1880's. It is obvious that this particular type of American literary realism has

[1] Harry Levin, in "What Is Realism?" (*Contexts of Criticism* [New York: Atheneum, 1963], pp. 69–70), suggests that "perhaps, like students of the diverging 'romanticisms,' we should pluralize our subject"; and he quotes Karl Mannheim to the same effect: "Realism means different things in different contexts." In a discussion which considers the problem of definition in relation to romanticism, René Wellek passes on an appropriate warning from Valéry: "It is impossible to think seriously with words such as Classicism, Romanticism, Humanism, or Realism. One cannot get drunk or quench one's thirst with labels on a bottle" ("Romanticism Re-examined," *Romanticism Reconsidered: Selected Papers from the English Institute*, ed. Northrop Frye [New York: Columbia University Press, 1963], p. 111).

[2] *The Rise of the Novel: Studies in Defoe, Richardson and Fielding* (Berkeley, Calif.: University of California Press, 1962). See esp. pp. 11 and 32.

important affinities—whether they be encompassing, over-lapping, or merely tangential—with other kinds of realism. But before attempting a universal definition of realism, if such is useful or even possible, it seems profitable to discriminate among realisms and to consider closely the realism which comes into focus in America around 1885—a realism which is significant in world literature and crucial to an understanding of almost all subsequent American literature. In literary criticism as in biology, the dissection of individuals precedes the identification of species.

Having limited the scope of our definition to the 1880's in America, we must now divest ourselves of some of the traditional clichés of American literary history. In spite of Howells' perceptive observation that "our literature has always been distinguished by two tendencies, apparently opposite, but probably parallel," it has been conventional to see late nineteenth-century American literature as two literatures: one which turns east and one which turns west (Canby); one of palefaces and one of redskins (Rahv); a literature which has an "East-West geographical division, with the line of demarcation following the Allegheny Mountain range of the Eastern coast" (Spiller).[3] This convention has its usefulness, but it also generates a distortion, endlessly perpetuated in the textbooks and surveys, which forces Henry James and Mark Twain into separate, irreconcilable camps: Mark Twain with the men of the West, James with the ladies of the East. Professor Spiller's mountain-range demarcation is especially unfortunate, for it underscores with great force—tangibly almost—the misleadingly simplistic concept found in his Preface to *The Cycle of American Literature* (p. viii), in which Whitman, Mel-

---

[3] W. D. Howells, "Editor's Study," *Harper's Monthly*, LXXXIII (November 1891), 964; Robert E. Spiller, *The Cycle of American Literature* (New York: New American Library, 1957), p. 92. See also Henry Seidel Canby, *Turn West, Turn East: Mark Twain and Henry James* (Boston: Houghton Mifflin Co., 1951); and Philip Rahv, "Paleface and Redskin," *Image and Idea*, rev. and enl. ed. (New York: New Directions, 1957).

ville, Twain, and Dreiser are described as "more deeply American" than such writers as Irving, Longfellow, Lowell, and Howells—and James, by implication. Differently American perhaps, but surely not "more deeply." The view of James as somehow not very "American," a view vigorously and polemically asserted by Van Wyck Brooks and V. L. Parrington, has been a serious obstacle to a balanced and a total view of the American realistic movement.[4] The usual linear relationship, which depicts Mark Twain on the left, James on the right, and Howells in the middle, is perhaps more accurately seen as a triangle whose center, in 1885, is realism. There are many obvious differences between Twain and James, although some of these are largely superficial —matters of taste, dress, architecture, writing habits, and dinner companions. And it is true that James and Twain did not appreciate each other's work or recognize their common ground.[5] But what now needs to be emphasized is

[4] See Brooks, *The Pilgrimage of Henry James* (New York: E. P. Dutton & Co., 1925) and Parrington, *The Beginnings of Critical Realism in America: 1860–1920*, vol. III of *Main Currents in American Thought* (New York: Harcourt, Brace & Co., 1930), esp. pp. 239–241. Cf. Professor Spiller's comment in *The Cycle of American Literature* (p. 132), that "it was through the rejection of his times and his society that he [James] became the spectator and analyst rather than the recorder. His alienation was both from the America of his birth and from the changing concepts and values of the mid-nineteenth century." In a later section, warmed at the fire of James' art, Professor Spiller recants to some extent: "The back-trail of rejection had led into the heart of the American experience" (p. 142).

[5] "Did not appreciate" is perhaps too mild a phrase. Mark Twain wrote to Howells concerning *The Bostonians*, "I would rather be damned to John Bunyan's heaven than read that" (*Mark Twain–Howells Letters*, ed. Henry Nash Smith and William M. Gibson [Cambridge, Mass.: Harvard University Press, 1960], II, 534). At a rare meeting James is supposed to have asked Twain: "Do you know Bret Harte?" Twain's answer must have been calculated to put both the subject of the question and the questioner into proper perspective: "Yes, I know the son of a bitch" (*Mr. Dooley Remembers*, ed. Philip Dunne [Boston: Little, Brown & Co., 1963], p. 244).

their many literary similarities: their rejection of omniscient narration, their experimentation with point of view and a language appropriate to the central consciousness, their anti-romanticism, their moral commitment, their humor and satire, their condemnation of American materialism (James' *American Scene* in many ways is a rewriting of Twain's *Gilded Age*), and their ultimate faith in style and art. One can certainly make a case for Mark Twain as a redskin and James as a paleface, but what is often ignored is that, in 1885, they are fighting on the same side.

The redskin-paleface theory of American literature not only understates the relation between Twain and James, it also overstates the contribution of the West to realism. While it is true that the free and easy spirit of western mining camps, Mississippi barges, and cowboy campfires had an important influence on the fictional uses of contemporary settings and vernacular language (qualities which are not necessarily realistic but which contribute to the impetus toward realism), it is also true that the local color movement was just as strong in the East and South, as can be seen in the works of Sarah Orne Jewett, James Russell Lowell, Mary E. Wilkins Freeman, Joel Chandler Harris, and George Washington Cable. Since many critics seem geographically oriented, it might be observed that such writers as "Josh Billings," "Bill" Nye, "Artemus Ward," Thomas B. Thorpe, "John Phoenix," and Bret Harte all had eastern origins and did much of their writing and publishing in the East, where the most lucrative market for their works was found. It was the New York *Saturday Press* which first launched "Jim Smiley and His Jumping Frog," not the Virginia City *Daily Territorial Enterprise* or the Sacramento *Union*. T. B. Thorpe's famous "Big Bear of Arkansas" first appeared in the New York *Spirit of the Times*. And Mark Twain's *Innocents Abroad* received only faint praise from Bret Harte in the San Francisco *Overland Monthly* but was enthusiastically welcomed in the East by

Oliver Wendell Holmes and the young assistant editor of the *Atlantic Monthly*, W. D. Howells.[6]

The neglect of the literary relationships which link Mark Twain and James has contributed to another myopia in American literary criticism, the neglect of realism itself. Twain, James, and Howells, as individuals, have been closely studied, but their impact as a group and as a movement has often been ignored. Ironically, realism, which vigorously and relentlessly fought the materialism and superficialities of the late nineteenth century, has itself suffered from the historical mud which has been thrown, too easily, at the period which is variously labeled "the Gilded Age," "the Chromo Civilization," "the Age of Innocence," "the Victorian Period," "the Age of Accumulation," and "the Great Barbecue." The fact that Mark Twain named and damned the age is somehow written off, since many biographers, beguiled into amateur psychoanalysis, claim that Colonel Sellers is really a projection of one face of the Mr. Clemens–Mark Twain split personality.

The neglect of the realistic period has its roots in the literary revaluations of the early years of the twentieth century, revaluations that became rigidified in Vernon L. Parrington's *Main Currents in American Thought*. Parrington's attack on the "slovenly reality beneath the gaudy exterior" and his wholesale condemnation of an "uncouth generation" was a remarkable display of rhetorical fireworks:

There is reason in plenty for such caustic comment. Heedless, irreverent, unlovely, cultivating huge beards, shod in polished top-boots—the last refinement of the farmer's cowhides—wearing linen dickeys over hickory shirts, moving through pools of tobacco juice, erupting in shoddy and grotesque architecture, cluttering its homes with ungainly walnut chairs and marble-topped tables and heavy lambrequins, the decade of the seven-

[6] Justin Kaplan, *Mr. Clemens and Mark Twain* (New York: Simon & Schuster, 1966), pp. 107–108.

ties was only too plainly mired and floundering in a bog of bad taste.[7]

Realism, according to Parrington, was only mildly under way in the 1880's. "Conditions were not ripe for it." "American taste was still romantic. . . . For the American born before the Civil War . . . the traditional outlook on life was unchanged; he still clung to the old moralities, the old verities, the old faith in the goodness of life in America."[8] Parrington's biases are so obvious and honest, and at this date so antiquated, that it no longer seems necessary to belabor them. Nevertheless we should keep in mind the inadequacy of much of his criticism simply because of its widespread impact. According to Parrington, James is a "self-deceived romantic," Mark Twain is a "simple child of the frontier," and Howells, whose realism was presumably strangled by the genteel tradition, merely marks a "transition between the earlier idealism and the later naturalism."[9] In the violence of his attack on the nineteenth century Parrington fails to grasp the significance of American realism, which he seems to consider a kind of protonaturalism. *Main Currents in American Thought* also provides many examples of how overstatement often leads to inconsistency. After his vitriolic attack on the boorishness of the "drab, negative" Gilded Age, Parrington can still condemn Henry James for finding "that the American atmosphere was uncongenial to the artist."[10]

Parrington's party line has had many followers. Alfred Kazin, who on the whole has a much sounder view of Howells and James, still refers to the late nineteenth century as a "period of dark ignorance and repressive Victorian

[7] *Beginnings of Critical Realism*, p. 10. See H. Wayne Morgan's comments on Parrington and the age in *The Gilded Age: A Reappraisal* (Syracuse: Syracuse University Press, 1963), pp. 1–13.

[8] *Beginnings of Critical Realism*, pp. 237–239.

[9] *Ibid.*, pp. 240, 242, 253.

[10] *Ibid.*, p. 239.

gentility" which led to, but did not itself produce, an important American literature.[11] Many of the standard texts have followed suit. In the influential 1400 pages of *Literary History of the United States*, realism merits only three pages of a chapter on De Forest and Howells, which itself is sandwiched between "Western Record and Romance" and "Experiments in Poetry."[12] In the presumably definitive *Bibliography* to *Literary History of the United States*, the "Movements and Influences" section (pp. 245–370) covers such specialized topics as the literature of New Netherland, Indian captives, Abolitionist magazines, and the Overland Trail, but realism is omitted. The reader hunts in vain for discussions of realism in such well-known works as *The Theory of American Literature*, *The American Adam*, and *Symbolism and American Literature*.[13] Surveys of American literature—those by Van Doren and Wagenknecht are characteristic[14]—tend to discuss realism briefly in a paragraph or two concerning the local colorists, to mention John De Forest as an "early realist," and to devote the remainder of a chapter to Howells, as the outstanding exemplar of a realism which is never usefully defined. Clarence Gohdes, in his section of A. H. Quinn's *The Literature of the American People*, summarizes what has too often been the standard approach to nineteenth-century American realism. In a two-page discussion prior to the inevitable consideration of De Forest and Howells, Professor Gohdes states that we may as well set aside "any consistent philosophy or attitude

[11] *On Native Grounds* (Garden City, N.Y.: Doubleday & Co., 1956), p. vii.

[12] *Literary History of the United States: History*, ed. R. E. Spiller, Willard Thorpe, T. H. Johnson, and H. S. Canby, 3d ed. rev. (New York: Macmillan Co., 1963; orig. pub. 1948).

[13] By Howard Mumford Jones (Ithaca, N.Y.: Cornell University Press, 1948), R. W. B. Lewis, (Chicago: University of Chicago Press, 1955), and Charles Feidelson, Jr. (Chicago: University of Chicago Press, 1953).

[14] Carl Van Doren, *The American Novel, 1789–1939*, rev. and enl. ed. (New York: Macmillan Co., 1940); Edward Wagenknecht, *Cavalcade of the American Novel* (New York: Henry Holt & Co., 1952).

of a realistic sort which may have been the possession of various authors of the period, for there are few such authors to be found in the century. . . ."[15] In a recent publication of the National Council of Teachers of English, *The Teacher and American Literature* (1965), William Peden claims that modern short fiction stems from Sherwood Anderson, whose *Winesburg, Ohio* was "a declaration of literary independence":

Anderson rejected romantic excess, contrivance, improbability, overemphasis on mechanical plotting, sentimentality, artificiality, and the one-dimensional caricatures or cardboard cutouts . . . far removed from reality and unconcerned with art. Anderson strove for truth as he saw it; he sought his materials—or they sought and found him—in the lives of nonexceptional people in unspectacular surroundings; he shifted his focus from the recording of external events to the analysis and depiction of what lay "beneath the surface of lives."[16]

[15] Clarence Gohdes in "Realism for the Middle Class," *The Literature of the American People: An Historical and Critical Survey*, ed. A. H. Quinn (New York: Appleton-Century-Crofts, 1951), p. 661. Professor Gohdes' attitude is conveyed by his subtitle in the table of contents: "Signs of a small trend toward realism."

[16] "Recent Developments in the American Short Story," p. 36. Professor Peden has high praise for William Faulkner, but he ignores Faulkner's opinion that the literary "father" of Sherwood Anderson was Mark Twain. See Faulkner's "A Note on Sherwood Anderson" (originally published as "Sherwood Anderson: An Appreciation"), *Essays, Speeches and Public Letters*, ed. James B. Meriwether (New York: Random House, 1965), p. 5. A more subtle heresy concerning the literary achievements of the realists is summarized by Quentin Anderson in his Foreword to Warner Berthoff's *The Ferment of Realism: American Literature, 1884–1919* (New York: Free Press, 1965), p. viii: "Mr. Berthoff does a fresh and admirable job of outlining the curious imbalance of intellectual and creative energy in this particular period—acknowledging for the first time in a 'literary' history what we had all along known but had hardly reckoned with —the fact that its novels are not only not as exciting as the work of William James, Thorstein Veblen, or Henry Adams, but are actually to be subsumed under the work of the thinkers of the period."

Without realizing it, Professor Peden has given us a very accurate definition of the aims and achievement of the realists in the mid-1880's, and his failure to mention James, Mark Twain, or Howells is characteristic of the critical neglect which realism has suffered.

CHAPTER III

PREVIOUS DEFINITIONS OF AMERICAN REALISM

IN SPITE of widespread critical neglect, there have been attempts to define American realism ever since the term gained currency, and notoriety, in the 1880's. Most of these attempts, in one way or another, start with the campaign for realism conducted by W. D. Howells in the "Editor's Study" in *Harper's Monthly*, a feature which Howells initiated in January, 1886. In these essays, abbreviated and rearranged for *Criticism and Fiction* in 1891, Howells constantly campaigned for fiction that was true to life, that dealt with everyday experiences in ordinary lives, that examined character and abandoned the "effectism" of narrative contortions and emotional outbursts. His phrases, repeated for eight decades, now have the worn and comfortable surface of antique coins: "Realism is nothing more and nothing less than the truthful treatment of material"; "We must ask ourselves before we ask anything else, Is it true?—true to the motives, the impulses, the principles that shape the life of actual men and women?"; "Let fiction cease to lie about life; let it portray men and women as they are . . . let it speak the dialect, the language, that most Americans know."[1]

Although Howells' phrases seem somewhat generalized today, there was little problem concerning the definition of realism in the 1880's. Howells and James had a clear real-

---

[1] *Harper's Monthly*, LXXIX (November 1889), 966; LXXIV (April 1887), 826; LXXIV (May 1887), 987. (*Harper's* full title in the 1880's was *Harper's New Monthly Magazine*, shortened to *Harper's Monthly Magazine* in 1900, and to *Harper's Magazine* in 1919.)

ization of the revolutionary character of the new fiction, and they elaborated the theories of their practice in the hundreds of letters, essays, and reviews which mark the beginning of American literary criticism as a serious genre. Their opponents apparently also had a clear understanding of realism, for the argument in the 1880's did not concern what realism was, but whether it was to be praised or condemned, largely in moral terms. The argument was based upon a fundamental disagreement concerning the purpose of fiction. Should the novel hold the mirror up to nature or should it "lighten the burdens of life by taking us for a time out of our humdrum and perhaps sordid conditions, so that we can see familiar life somewhat idealized," as Charles Dudley Warner claimed in the *Atlantic Monthly* in 1883.[2] A more impassioned critic, Maurice Thompson, stated that fiction should "imagine noble instances of human self-sacrifice, of lofty aspiration and of soul-stirring passion"—a concise summary of the qualities which the realists detested.[3] Henry James expressed the conflict succinctly in his miniaturized household version of the nineteenth-century realism war— "The Author of *Beltraffio*" (1884). Mark Ambient's statements of his critical theory ("I want to give an impression of life itself . . . filled with the purest distillation of the actual. . . . I care for seeing things as they are") could pass for one of Howells' contributions to the "Editor's Study." His wife Beatrice, using the arguments of the critics of realism, finds his work purposeless and immoral. "Her conception of a novel," Ambient complains, "is a thing so false that it makes me blush. It is a thing so hollow, so dishonest, so lying, in which life is so blinked and blinded, so dodged and disfigured, that it makes my ears burn. It's two different ways of looking at the whole affair."[4]

[2] LI (April 1883), 469.

[3] Originally published in the Chicago *Sunday Times*; quoted by Herbert Edwards, "Howells and the Controversy over Realism in American Fiction," *American Literature*, III (November 1931), 239.

[4] *The Complete Tales of Henry James*, ed. Leon Edel (Philadelphia: J. B. Lippincott Co., 1962–64), V, 331–336.

Led by Howells, the "New Literature" (as the *Century Magazine* liked to call realism) stamped hard on transcendental toes, calling forth vigorous protests from the defenders of idealism, sentimentality, and romance. For the post-Mencken reader, overly familiar with the charges of prudery, tame geniality, and pressed violets that have been brought against the man who wrote about the smiling aspects of life for sheltered young girls, it comes as something of a surprise to find Howells roasted by his contemporaries for his shocking subject matter and his vulgar tone. In November, 1885, an anonymous reviewer for the *Catholic World* found *The Rise of Silas Lapham* a decadent and immoral novel which "out-Zolas Zola." Others found Howells' work a "corrupting influence," "hopeless," distinguished for "vulgarity," and a blight upon the "germs of spirituality." These critics would have had some difficulty recognizing the Dean as painted by Sinclair Lewis in his waspish Nobel Prize Address in 1930: "Mr. Howells was one of the gentlest, sweetest and most honest of men and had the code of a pious old maid whose greatest delight is to have tea at the vicarage." Both of these views, like most of the variously motivated attacks on Howells, tell us more about the vagaries of American intellectual history than about Howells' art and criticism.[5]

"The war of the critics over William Dean Howells," as Professors Cady and Frazier have shown in their anthology, subtly shifts its ground from the contemporary attack or defense of Howells' championship of realism to later attacks on his conservatism, and finally to the larger considerations of Howells' artistry, realism itself, and the role of realism

---

[5] See "Novel Writing as a Science," *Catholic World*, XLII (November 1885), 274–280; Lewis' address was printed in full by the New York *Times* on 13 December 1930, p. 12. See also Edwin H. Cady, *The Road to Realism: The Early Years, 1837–1885, of William Dean Howells* (Syracuse: Syracuse University Press, 1956), pp. 240–243; and *The Realist at War: The Mature Years, 1885–1920, of William Dean Howells* (Syracuse: Syracuse University Press, 1958), pp. 1–55; cf. Edwards, "Howells and the Controversy over Realism."

in American literary history. The war of the critics is still being fought by a number of modern scholars who have joined the battle over the definition of American realism. Gordon Haight, in a brief discussion which suggests both the international aspects of nineteenth-century realism and its relationship to romanticism, defines the realists' aim as "an accurate, objective reproduction of scene and character for its own sake."[6] James D. Hart agrees that realism "aims at an interpretation of the actualities of any aspect of life, free from subjective prejudice, idealism or romantic color,"[7] a definition that is elaborated by Professor Thrall and Dean Hibbard: "The realist espouses what is essentially a mimetic theory of art, centering his attention in the thing imitated and asking for something close to a one-to-one correspondence between the representation and the subject." The realist, according to this interpretation, writes with "absolute truthfulness."[8] This emphasis on the conformity of realism to fact is also seen in Lars Åhnebrink's *The Beginnings of Naturalism in American Fiction*: "*Realism* is a manner and method of composition by which the author describes *normal, average life* in an accurate and truthful way."[9]

George Becker, in an extensive and thoughtful consideration, starts from much the same premise: the primary goal of realism is "the truthful representation of observable fact with emphasis upon the norm of experience"; it is "a faithful reproduction of 'real' life."[10] Professor Becker divides

[6] "Realism Defined: William Dean Howells," *Literary History of the United States: History*, ed. R. E. Spiller *et al.*, 3d ed., rev. (New York: Macmillan Co., 1963), p. 878.

[7] *The Oxford Companion to American Literature*, 4th ed. (New York: Oxford University Press, 1965), p. 698.

[8] William F. Thrall and Addison Hibbard, *A Handbook to Literature*, rev. and enl. ed. by C. Hugh Holman (New York: Odyssey Press, 1960), pp. 397–398.

[9] Upsala University Essays and Studies on American Language and Literature, vol. IX (Cambridge, Mass.: Harvard University Press, 1950), p. vi.

[10] "Realism: An Essay in Definition," *Modern Language Quarterly*,

realism into method (carefully observed and objective details of common experience), subject matter (the average and lower social levels), and philosophy (pessimistic determinism) and makes high claims for factual and objective presentation: "The realist has . . . an accuracy of external detail and a passion for fact in the representation of the external aspects of behavior and environment which lend an air of absolute validity to fiction, making it no longer a feigned thing; . . . he serves no interest; he has no preconceived views of how things should be; he observes and states. . . . The basic ideal of the movement was and is absolute objectivity."[11] Leaning heavily on realism's local color roots, Marcus Cunliffe states that " 'realism,' then, entailed writing about the environment one knew, with strict regard to its actual properties—speech, dress, scene, behavior."[12] Warner Berthoff leans in the other direction chronologically, coupling realism and naturalism, but his definition of the "premise" of realism corresponds to Cunliffe's: "the work of capturing the special immediate air of American reality in the familiar American dialect."[13]

Many of these critical positions were restated recently by the participants in Conference 6 ("Discussion of Key Terms") at the 1967 Modern Language Association meeting in Chicago. The conferees, in a follow-up questionnaire conducted by *American Literary Realism* editor Clayton Eichelberger, tended to define realism in terms of six frequently mentioned characteristics: "fidelity to actuality, objectivity (or neutrality—the absence of authorial judgment), democratic focus (particularized, ordinary characters), social

---

X (June 1949), 194, 187. Professor Becker's Introduction to *Documents of Modern Literary Realism* (Princeton, N.J.: Princeton University Press, 1963) repeats and elaborates his earlier discussion.

[11] "Realism: An Essay in Definition," pp. 186, 188, 192.

[12] "Realism in American Prose," *The Literature of the United States* (Baltimore: Penguin Books, 1961), p. 187.

[13] *The Ferment of Realism: American Literature, 1884–1919* (New York: Free Press, 1965), p. 2.

awareness (and critical appraisal), reportorial detail, and colloquial expression."[14]

The difficulty with these and similar definitions is that they depend on a small, often-repeated group of singularly evasive words—"truth," "actuality," "accuracy," "reality," "objectivity." These words often raise more problems than they solve, and they are difficult to apply specifically to works of the imagination. Inherent in such definitions are three misleading ideas which have gained an unfortunate currency in discussions of American realism:

1. Realism uses realistic details (or, as some critics prefer, verisimilitude). The implication is that writing that is not "realistic" does not use such details.
2. Realism is the presentation of reality, the truth about experience.
3. Realism is objective, and makes no judgment upon its materials.

Each of these clichés must be considered before the way will be clear for a new approach to the definition of American realism.

Discussions of realism have long been sidetracked by an excessive attention to what are called "realistic details"— those concrete glimpses of the facts of common life which provide a shock of recognition for every reader. Critics endlessly point to specific facts, reportorial research, historically accurate events, and recognizable geographic places in realistic fiction, claiming that the realist has a "belief in fact as a way to truth"[15] and a "reverence for the material surface of things,"[16] and that he "uses detached observation and relies on specific facts."[17] Realism's etymological parent,

[14] "Mostly Relevant," *American Literary Realism: 1870–1910*, no. 3 (Summer 1968), p. 74.

[15] Becker, "Realism: An Essay in Definition," p. 192.

[16] Everett Carter, *Howells and the Age of Realism* (Philadelphia: J. B. Lippincott Co., 1954), p. 21.

[17] H. Wayne Morgan, *American Writers in Rebellion* (New York: Hill & Wang, 1965), p. vii.

Latin *res* ("thing"), is often pointed out in order to suggest a family resemblance. This emphasis on the details used by the realists overlooks an obvious point: every writer uses "realistic" details. Homer tells his reader how to wash clothes, how to prepare a heifer for sacrifice, and how to build a ship.[18] Dante's lost souls, bodiless as they are, suffer vivid physical torments which still tingle the spines of modern readers. The "realism" of the Wife of Bath, the Miller, and the Reeve is invariably discussed in introductions, as is the realism of Dogberry, Mistress Quickly, Juliet's nurse, and the citizens in *Coriolanus* and *Julius Caesar*, with their strong breath and sweaty nightcaps. "Realism" used in this general way almost always refers to realistic details, which, in some measure, are present in every literary work. (What detail in the history of literature and drama could be more "realistic" than the discharge of cannon in *King Henry the Eighth* which burned the Globe theatre to the ground on June 29, 1613?)

Realistic details do not define realism because of their widespread and continual use, and also because of their special employment by romantic writers, who use such details to lead the reader gradually, plausibly, into worlds of transcendental spirit or impossible fantasy.[19] The romantic poets, following Wordsworth's prefatory dictum in *Lyrical*

---

[18] Homer's precision in the details of shipbuilding has been verified by the recent discovery of a Bronze Age merchant ship. See Peter Throckmorton, "Thirty-three Centuries under the Sea" and "Oldest Known Shipwreck Yields Bronze Age Cargo," *National Geographic*, vols. 117 (May 1960) and 121 (May 1962). The detailed, externalized Homeric style is perceptively discussed by Erich Auerbach in the "Odysseus' Scar" chapter of *Mimesis*, trans. Willard Trask (Princeton, N.J.: Princeton University Press, 1953).

[19] In his Introduction to *Miss Ravenel's Conversion* (New York: Holt, Rinehart & Winston, 1955), p. vi, Gordon Haight notes that "[Realism] should not be considered the antithesis of romance, for realism was actually developed by the romancers to make their creations plausible." Haight is presumably talking about realistic details, and "actually developed" seems too strong, but his point is important.

Ballads to look steadily at their subjects, have built countless poems upon precise naturalistic description. The maca-
bre effect of Poe's tales is based in large part upon the
juxtaposition of homely details and grotesque horror. Poe
introduces "The Black Cat," a narrative of animal atrocity
and uxoricide, with an ironic bit of Howellsian editorializing: "My immediate purpose is to place before the world,
plainly, succinctly, and without comment, a series of mere
household events."[20] Chapter for chapter, romanticist Walter Scott uses many more realistic details than realist Henry
James. This romantic technique is well summarized by John
Ruskin in *Modern Painters*: "In the representation of the
Heroic or Impossible forms, the greatest care must be taken
in *finishing the details*."[21]

It is obvious that the realists themselves employ realistic
details to achieve the "air of reality (solidity of specification)" which James called "the supreme virtue of a novel,"[22]
but since such usage is not peculiar to the realists, it is a
sandy base upon which to build a definition. In addition,
Howells, James, and Twain all deny the significance of
mere details and a one-to-one correspondence between the
subject and the representation. Howells is very clear on this
point: "When realism becomes false to itself, when it heaps
up facts merely, and maps life instead of picturing it, realism will perish too."[23] More playfully, Mark Twain, who
could "remember anything, whether it had happened or
not,"[24] discusses in his *Autobiography* his technique of
adjusting facts and details to the requirements of imagina-

[20] *The Complete Poems and Stories of Edgar Allan Poe*, ed. A. H.
Quinn and E. H. O'Neill (New York: Alfred A. Knopf, 1951), I, 476.

[21] *The Works of John Ruskin*, ed. E. T. Cook and Alexander Wed-
derburn (New York: Longmans, Green & Co., 1904), V, 33.

[22] "The Art of Fiction," *Longman's Magazine*, IV (September 1884),
510.

[23] "Editor's Study," *Harper's Monthly*, LXXII (May 1886), 973.

[24] *The Autobiography of Mark Twain*, ed. Charles Neider (New
York: Harper & Row, 1959), p. 3.

tive fiction. As a boy Sam Clemens spent his summers on his uncle's farm near Florida, Missouri, a farm that became "very handy . . . in literature":

In *Huck Finn* and in *Tom Sawyer, Detective* I moved it down to Arkansas. It was all of six hundred miles but it was no trouble; it was not a very large farm—five hundred acres, perhaps—but I could have done it if it had been twice as large. And as for the morality of it, I cared nothing for that; I would move a state if the exigencies of literature required it.[25]

In January, 1885, Howells took issue with overly "accurate minds" and carefully explained the realists' position concerning literally precise details and the relation between specific facts and general truth. He had been accused of "anachronism" for his reference to Daisy Miller in the first installment of *The Rise of Silas Lapham* in the November, 1884, issue of the *Century Magazine*. In the opening chapter Bartley Hubbard's article on Colonel Lapham described Lapham's wife Persis as "one of those women who, in whatever walk of life, seem born to honor the name of American Woman, and to redeem it from the national reproach of Daisy Millerism."[26] A few pages earlier Lapham had remarked that "this is '75," and a reader noted that "Daisy Miller" was first published in the *Cornhill Magazine* in 1878. Howells replied in the *Century*'s "Open Letters" section:

As I may hereafter repeat this cause of offense to accurate minds, perhaps it will be well for me to state the principle upon which I reconcile it to a conscience not void of the usual anxiety. It appears to me that I discharge my whole duty to reality in giving, as well as I can, the complexion of the period of which I write, and I would as lief as not allow one of my persons to speak of Daisy Millerism, even a whole year before Daisy Miller

[25] *Ibid.*, p. 4. "I don't believe these details are right," Twain once wrote, "but I don't care a rap. They will do just as well as the facts" (p. xv).

[26] P. 20.

appeared in print, if it gave a characteristic tint in the portraiture. In like manner I would make bold to use a type-writer in 1875, when it had only come into the market in 1874; and if an electric light threw a more impressive glare upon certain aspects of life than the ordinary gas-burner, I should have no hesitation in anticipating the inventions of Mr. Edison several months.

An artist illustrating my story would put the people in the fashions of 1884, though they actually dressed in those of 1875, and I think he would be right; for it is the effect of contemporaneousness that is to be given, and the general truth is sometimes better than the specific fact.[27]

A second misleading idea that has impeded discussions of realism is the notion that somehow realism is closer to reality, to "real life," than other kinds of writing—as if the globes of fiction actually could hold the vasty fields of France. This slice-of-life approach ignores the fact that all writing is mimetic, that "the only reason for the existence of a novel is that it does attempt to represent life."[28] The choice open to the writer is not whether to represent life, but rather how it might be represented. Every work ultimately is related to the realities of the human condition, and every writer represents the world as he sees it. Such principles have not only become commonplaces for the twentieth-century author, they have themselves become topics for literature.

[27] XXIX (January 1885), 477. The misplaced emphasis on details can perhaps be seen by following its implications to the extreme. Many of the comments about the "accuracy of external detail" of the nineteenth-century realists might be much more appropriately applied to such recent works as Truman Capote's *In Cold Blood* and the partially tape-recorded *La Vida* by Oscar Lewis. These books rely heavily on massive realistic detail, and although they can perhaps be seen as great-grandchildren of nineteenth-century realism, they clearly do not represent the realistic sensibility which produced the novels and stories of the mid-1880's.

[28] Henry James, "The Art of Fiction," *Partial Portraits* (London: Macmillan & Co., 1888), p. 378. James' rewording of this sentence is significant. In the original version published in *Longman's Magazine*, it read: "The only reason for the existence of a novel is that it *does* compete with life" (IV [September 1884], 503).

Reality, as Wallace Stevens suggests, depends upon the color of one's guitar.

Blue guitars did not exist for nineteenth-century idealists, who tried to defeat realism semantically by inverting the term and insisting, with Emerson, that only the ideal is real.[29] John Burroughs, in a chapter entitled "The True Realism," stated that "it is only the idealist who can adequately deal with the real," because real things "are only a means to an end, and that end is not the literal truth, but the ideal truth."[30] Charles F. Richardson maintained that a "true realism has portrayed men and women as they are—creatures with souls." True realism, according to Richardson, "remembered that life has its color and romance as well as its dun tameness, and that from its wood and ashes the fire of aspiration flames up toward the ideal."[31] A more philosophical critic, Hamilton Wright Mabie, saw the problem clearly in his review of *The Rise of Silas Lapham*. The realists, Mabie contended, have redefined reality. They dissent not merely from a particular literary method but from the older belief in the reality of spiritual types and universal facts. They deny "the existence in nature of the . . . essential reality of the old ends and subjects of art."[32]

These shifting uses of "reality" have been pawns in a longstanding and essentially pointless argument between realism and romanticism, an argument in which the question of reality becomes merged with the question of truth. In discussing Queequeg's native home of Kokovoko, Melville

[29] See Emerson's "Idealism," part vi of *Nature*, esp. section 2. This is the basic position of the medieval "realists," who, following Plato's doctrines, were actually idealists and universalists. Philosophy has treated the term "realism" with even more confusion than literature has, a confusion that itself argues against single-minded interpretations of "reality."

[30] *Indoor Studies* (Boston: Houghton, Mifflin & Co., 1889), pp. 231, 234.

[31] *American Literature: 1607–1885* (New York: G. P. Putnam's Sons, 1888), II, 415–416.

[32] "A Typical Novel," *Andover Review*, IV (November 1885), 425.

noted that "it is not down in any map; true places never are."[33] Howells, if he had read *Moby-Dick*, would have seen this kind of statement as characteristic of the "fantastic romance" which belongs in the category of mere "decorative arts," lacking the truth of "works that represent and body forth human experience."[34] Which then is more "true," more "real," the romantic leap at the heart of the universe or the realistic portrayal of the average lot? No answer to this question is possible, and none is necessary. Human experience has its claims; so do those moods which need "heaven, hell, purgatory, and faeryland for their expression, no less than this dilapidated earth."[35] There is the truth of the world of common experience and the truth of uncommon worlds apart; the truth of the day and the truth of the night. The romantics sought the Melvillian night ("darkness were indeed the proper element of our essences") or the Hawthornian twilight ("where the Actual and the Imaginary may meet"); the realists simply preferred to deal with ordinary experience under a bright Howellsian sun ("It must be treated in no lurid twilight gloom, but in plain, simple, matter-of-fact noonday").[36] But the two kinds of fiction, as De Forest wrote to Howells in December, 1886, "are equally allowable and in a certain sense equally true.

[33] *Moby-Dick*, ed. Charles Feidelson, Jr. (Indianapolis: Bobbs-Merrill Co., 1964), p. 88.

[34] "Editor's Study," *Harper's Monthly*, LXXII (May 1886), 972–973.

[35] W. B. Yeats, "A Teller of Tales," *The Celtic Twilight* (London: A. H. Bullen, 1902), p. 7. The remainder of the passage well expresses the antirealistic position: "Nay, are there not moods which shall find no expression unless there be men who dare to mix heaven, hell, purgatory, and faeryland together, or even to set the heads of beasts to the bodies of men, or to thrust the souls of men into the heart of rocks? Let us go forth, the tellers of tales, and seize whatever prey the heart long for, and have no fear. Everything exists, everything is true, and the earth is only a little dust under our feet."

[36] *Moby-Dick*, p. 87; *The Scarlet Letter*, ed. Larzer Ziff (text of the Centenary Edition; Indianapolis: Bobbs-Merrill Co., 1963), p. 36; *The Shadow of a Dream and An Imperative Duty*, ed. E. H. Cady (New Haven, Conn.: College & University Press, 1962), p. 227.

Each is the result of a selection; for we cannot tell the whole life."[37]

Although there has been much confusion about "truth" and about "reality" in discussions of realism, several scholars have recently helped to clarify the issue. Harry Levin bypasses the problem of defining reality "since it cannot bear precisely the same significance for any two human beings."[38] Marcus Cunliffe also refuses to become enmeshed in the entangling problems raised by such terms as "real life" and "reality," since "they beg the question of what is meant by *life* or *reality*."[39] Professor Spiller points out that realism for James (and he could be speaking of all the realists) is a matter of representing life as the author sees it, "which may not be the same as life as it 'really' is."[40] Edwin Cady takes it a conclusive step further: " 'Realism' is neither more nor less 'real' than any other kind of successful literary art."[41]

The confusion concerning "reality" in discussions of realism has been accompanied by a similar confusion over "objectivity." The two problems are related, for an objective account of experience presumably would capture reality. George Becker makes precisely this claim for the realists. Since "the basic ideal of the movement was and is absolute objectivity," the realist, in Professor Becker's view, is able to achieve a "truthful representation of observable fact," that is, reality.[42] This doctrine may appear reasonable when applied to novelistic technique, and Professor Becker per-

[37] James F. Light, *John William De Forest* (New York: Twayne Publishers, 1965), p. 167.

[38] "What Is Realism?" *Contexts of Criticism* (New York: Atheneum, 1963), p. 68.

[39] *Literature of the United States*, p. 187.

[40] *The Cycle of American Literature* (New York: New American Library, 1957), p. 134. James might add that life as one sees it *is* life as it "really" is.

[41] *Road to Realism*, p. 159.

[42] "Realism: An Essay in Definition," pp. 192, 194.

ceptively notes the realists' tendency to reject the role of the authorial commentator and to rely on scenes and dialogue for narrative development (the "dramatic method," in James' phraseology). But Professor Becker illustrates the fundamental fallacy of the doctrine of objectivity when he states that the realist takes "great pains not to allow any personal prejudice or predilection to divert him from presenting things as they are. . . . At his best [the realist] serves no interest; he has no preconceived views of how things should be; he observes and he states." Thus when the realist commits himself to a cause, to a purpose, to an opinion, he is "thereby almost necessarily compromising his objectivity" and "realism ends."[43]

It is difficult to find a book which would fulfill this definition of realism. What author writes without purpose, cause, or opinion? The realistic novels of the 1880's come immediately to mind, with Mark Twain's attack on contemporary religion, politics, morality, culture, and whatever else he could think of, and his defense of the humanity of the Negro; James' satire on feminism, the Boston reform movement, and, less obviously, the postwar South; and Howells' double-barreled destruction of both business and Brahminism, his unrelenting antisentimentality, and his development of the doctrine of complicity. "Absolute objectivity" is relatively impossible.

While the realists do not achieve or even attempt to achieve absolute objectivity, they do strive for the illusion of objectivity, an illusion that was ignored by many eight-

[43] *Ibid.*, pp. 187–188. Becker's article is quoted at length because of the clarity of its exposition. Many other critics share his opinions. Gordon Haight, for example, speaks of the "complete objectivity" of De Forest ("Realism Defined," p. 881). Becker's notion that social theory is incompatible with realism becomes more useful as the social theory becomes more dogmatic and rigidified, and is certainly valid at the extreme of "socialist realism," which, as Harry Levin has remarked, is a contradiction in terms ("What Is Realism?" p. 75). In fairness, it should be noted that Professor Becker allows that the maintenance of objectivity is "extremely difficult" (p. 188).

eenth- and early nineteenth-century novelists. The fiction of Fielding, Trollope, and Dickens is often analogous to a puppet show. One can see both the characters and the puppeteer who makes them move. Many modern writers and critics, such men as Percy Lubbock, Ford Madox Ford, and Hemingway, claim that successful modern fiction, following the lead of the realists, is objective. Characters move by themselves on the stage and there is no puppeteer. This, I think, is overenthusiastic nonsense. Fiction is still a puppet show, still an illusion of life. The difference, largely introduced by the realists, is that a frame and covering have been built around the fictional stage. The puppeteer and the mechanism are now hidden, although the wires are still visible if one looks closely. As Wayne Booth has reminded us, "We must never forget that though the author can to some extent choose his disguises, he can never choose to disappear."[44]

[44] *The Rhetoric of Fiction* (Chicago: University of Chicago Press, 1961), p. 20.

CHAPTER IV

AMERICAN REALISM DEFINED

"REALISM," according to the *Guide to the Study of the United States of America*, "is a semantic house of many mansions."[1] Having considered previous discussions of realism, we are now in a position to suggest a structural definition for that particular mansion which houses nineteenth-century American realism—a definition that is partially a synthesis of previous work and partially new. Identifying characteristics of the realistic writing which culminated in the mid-1880's can be found in four areas: philosophy, subject matter, morality, and style. These areas are, of course, finally inseparable, but considering each one individually gives us a convenient method for confronting the full dimensions of American realism.

The philosophy of American realism is not a philosophy in a specialized, technical sense, but rather a loosely organized and often generalized set of convictions and attitudes—an after-dinner brandy-and-cigars philosophy, rather than an epistemologically sound academic system. It is best introduced by first considering the beliefs of an earlier generation of writers, beliefs which the realists oppose and reject. In "The Poetic Principle," Poe maintains that art must reflect man's immortal search for higher beauty: "Inspired by an ecstatic prescience of the glories beyond the grave, we struggle by multiform combinations among the things and

---

[1] Washington: Library of Congress, 1960, p. 64.

thoughts of Time to attain a portion of that Loveliness whose very elements perhaps appertain to eternity alone."[2] Wordsworth states that the function of art is to "exhilarate the spirit," to reflect

> That most noble attribute of man . . .
> That wish for something loftier, more adorned,
> Than is the common aspect, daily garb,
> Of human life.[3]

Many romantic writers compose variations on a theme by Emerson—that succinct statement in *Nature* which is fundamental to romantic thought on both sides of the Atlantic: "Every natural fact is a symbol of some spiritual fact."[4] *trans* Carlyle, for example, finds that "all visible things are emblems; what thou seest is not there on its own account; strictly taken, is not there at all: Matter exists only spiritually, and to represent some Idea, and *body* it forth."[5] The implications of this romantic philosophy for literature were flatly summarized by Longfellow in *Kavanagh*, in 1849: "Literature is rather an image of the spiritual world than of the physical, is it not?"[6]

[2] *The Complete Poems and Stories of Edgar Allan Poe*, ed. A. H. Quinn and E. H. O'Neill (New York: Alfred A. Knopf, 1951), II, 1026. In an adjacent passage Poe considers, and rejects, the realistic sensibility: "He who shall simply sing, with however glowing enthusiasm, or with however vivid a truth of description, of the sights, and sounds, and odors, and colors, and sentiments, which greet *him* in common with all mankind—he, I say, has yet failed to prove his divine title."

[3] *The Prelude* (1850 ed.), ed. Ernest De Selincourt (London: Oxford University Press, 1926), pp. 141, 167 (bk. V, lines 108, 573, 575–577).

[4] *Selections from Ralph Waldo Emerson*, ed. Stephen E. Whicher (Boston: Houghton Mifflin Co., 1957), p. 32.

[5] *Sartor Resartus, The Works of Thomas Carlyle* (London: Chapman & Hall, 1896), I, 57 (bk. I, ch. 11).

[6] *Henry Wadsworth Longfellow: Prose Works* (Boston: Houghton, Mifflin & Co., 1904), II, 426. There is not space here to enter the controversy concerning the definition of romanticism—that is another war. But if the views of Peckham, Lovejoy, Wellek, Abrams, *et al.*

Separated by a generation from the romantics and by the greater gulf of Lyell's *Principles of Geology* (1830–33), Strauss' *Leben Jesu* (1835–36, translated by George Eliot in 1846), Darwin's *Origin of Species* (1859), Mill's *Utilitarianism* (1861), and Marx' *Das Kapital* (vol. I, 1867, translated 1886), the American realists answer Longfellow's question with a resounding no. They reject not only Poe's ideas but his entire vocabulary of "supernal Beauty," "immortal instinct," "crystal springs," "sublime angels," and "elevated souls." They deny Carlyle's definition of mankind—"light-sparkles floating in the æther of Deity!"[7] The philosophy of American realism, to borrow Carlyle's term, is "descendental," or, more accurately, nontranscendental. The realists cannot accept supernaturalism, Platonic idealism, and the worlds of spirit. They do not necessarily deny the validity of such worlds; they simply ignore them as unknowable in ordinary human terms and thus irrelevant to ordinary human experience. The American realists agreed with John Stuart Mill's formulation of the utilitarian position in his *Coleridge*:

We see no ground for believing that anything can be the object of our knowledge except our experience, and what can be inferred from our experience by the analogies of experience itself; nor that there is any idea, feeling or power in the human mind, which, in order to account for it, requires that its origin should be referred to any other source. . . . There is no knowledge *à*

---

are taken together, a central point does emerge. By almost every definition, romanticism involves a belief in a higher, transcendent, spiritual reality, which can inspire and transform men's lives. The realists cannot accept such superlunar reality, and in this respect, perhaps more than others, it is appropriate to speak of an opposition between romanticism and realism. See chapter 9, below.

[7] *Sartor Resartus*, p. 43 (bk. I, ch. 8). Scotty Briggs well expressed the realists' reaction to Carlyle's definition in his reply to the elegant statements of an Eastern clergyman: "You ruther hold over me, pard. I reckon I can't call that hand. Ante and pass the buck" (*Roughing It, The Writings of Mark Twain* [New York: Harper & Bros., 1929], IV, 45).

priori; no truths cognizable by the mind's inward light, and grounded on intuitive evidence.[8]

This unidealized view of human experience has an artistic corollary. The realists believe that the purpose of art, as always, is to instruct and to please—*aut prodesse aut delectare*. But the instruction and the pleasure lie in giving shape to life's meaning by seeing into human experience, rather than seeing through it to spirit, ideal, or godhead. It is not, as Hamilton Wright Mabie claimed, "practical atheism applied to art,"[9] but rather practical agnosticism applied to art. Mabie's nineteenth-century theological bias is clear, but there has been a more recent misunderstanding of the realists' position. The philosophical aspect of realism, according to George Becker, held that "life had no meaning, no telic motion, and that man was a creature barely escaped from the level of animal behavior and driven by forces over which he had no control and in which he could discern no purpose."[10] The basic problem here is the common confusion of realism and naturalism. The two movements are related, but they must be kept separate since they have very different attitudes toward human experience and society. In the mid-1880's the realists denied idealism without embracing pessimism; they rejected the affirmations of Longfellow and Tennyson without accepting the environmental web of Frank Norris and Thomas Hardy. In their best work the realists were pragmatic, relativistic, democratic, and experimental. They were not committed to dogmatic theories or fixed formulas, insisting only that fiction be true to life, that it be interesting, that it be honest, that it be the re-

[8] *On Bentham and Coleridge*, introd. F. R. Leavis (New York: Harper & Bros., 1962), pp. 114, 109.

[9] "A Typical Novel," *Andover Review*, IV (November 1885), 426. The *Andover Review* was subtitled *A Religious and Theological Monthly* and was edited by the faculty of the Andover Theological Seminary. Mabie was an editor for the *Christian Union*.

[10] "Realism: An Essay in Definition," *Modern Language Quarterly*, X (June 1949), 192.

sult of a direct impression of life. In 1885, the house of fiction had "not one window, but a million."[11]

The subject matter of the American realists in the 1880's provides another basis for definition, for all writers are defined to some extent by what they write about. The realistic subject matter is derived directly from the realistic philosophy. Subjects are drawn from "our experience, and what can be inferred from our experience by the analogies of experience itself."[12] The realists write about the common, the average, the unextreme, the representative, the probable. They concern themselves with ordinary human lives seen in the context of normal social relationships. They concentrate on what people are rather than what they ought to be, on men rather than Man. Much of the fiction written in the mid-1880's is topical: the Boston reform movement, feminism, the problem of the new American businessman, the European underground revolutionary movement. Most of the fiction deals with recognizable geographic locations— Boston's Beacon Street; Hannibal, Missouri; Cairo, Illinois; London's Buckingham Palace Road; the Ponte Vecchio in Florence.

Arguing from the "Editor's Study" in *Harper's*, Howells noted the difficulty of breaking the new literary ground of realistic subject matter and the resistance that it invariably caused. He went on to quote selected sections from Emerson's "The American Scholar" and "The Poet," excerpts which constitute an accurate definition of the subject matter of American realism:

[11] Henry James, Preface to *The Portrait of a Lady*, in *The Art of the Novel: Critical Prefaces*, ed. R. P. Blackmur (New York: Charles Scribner's Sons, 1934), p. 46. This preface and "The Art of Fiction" (1884) contain James' statements concerning the "direct impression of life." The latter is the best statement of the realists' belief in variety, freedom, and experimentation in fiction.

[12] *On Bentham and Coleridge*, p. 114.

I ask not for the great, the remote, the romantic. . . . I embrace
the common; I sit at the feet of the familiar and the low. . . . Man
is surprised to find that things near are not less beautiful and
wondrous than things remote. . . . The perception of the worth of
the vulgar is fruitful in discoveries. . . . The foolish man wonders
at the unusual, but the wise man at the usual. . . . To-day always
looks mean to the thoughtless; but to-day is a king in disguise.
. . . Banks and tariffs, the newspaper and caucus, Methodism and
Unitarianism, are flat and dull to dull people, but rest on the same
foundations of wonder as the town of Troy and the temple of
Delphos.[13]

Howells' quotations from Emerson were extracted with
some care, as the many ellipses indicate. Emerson does embrace the common, the familiar, and the low, but he also
sees these as emblems of the spiritual, as links to a higher
world. Howells, of course, breaks the links and denies the
emblems. What he carefully did not quote in these essays
tells as much about realism, by contrast, as what he did:
"Nature is a symbol"; "The near explains the far"; "The
Universe is the externalization of the soul"; "Each believes
himself inspired by the Divine Soul which also inspires all
men"; "I think nothing is of any value in books excepting
the transcendental and extraordinary"; "This is the reward;
that the ideal shall be real to thee, and the impressions of
the actual world shall fall like summer rain, copious, but not
troublesome to thy invulnerable essence."[14]

The Emersonian vocabulary—Divine Soul, transcendental, Universe, invulnerable essence—well represents those
aspects which the realists discard as subject matter. Their
rejection of the transcendental thus eliminates the wild
fantasies of the supernatural, the grotesque and the ara-
besque, the foreign and the strange, angels and devils, heroes
and villains. It denies the "everlasting itch for things remote," which motivates Ishmael in the first chapter of

13 LXXV (October 1887), 803.
14 *Selections from Emerson*, pp. 78, 80, 227, 236, 240.

Moby-Dick: "I love to sail forbidden seas, and land on barbarous coasts." Instead of barbarous coasts and great leviathans of the deep, flaming letters in the sky, or miraculous voices in the night, we have a makeshift Mississippi raft, the problems of a paint manufacturer, a meeting of disheveled reformers in Boston's South End. In 1885 the proper study of mankind was man.

The realists' concern with common experience, contemporary issues, and Baedeker topography should not lead us into the trap of discussing realism in terms of photographic portrayal, statistical norms, a one-to-one correspondence with reality, or a slice of life.[15] A slice of life, like a pound of flesh, is a messy affair. Fiction in the mid-1880's is still fictitious, and James, Howells, and Mark Twain do not choose their topics from raw and unrefined experience. The realists' representation of the common experience is ultimately achieved through imaginative realization rather than reportorial or statistical method. James' short tale, "The Real Thing," treats precisely this point. The artist of the story finds that truly genteel Major and Mrs. Monarch are unsatisfactory as models for illustrations of ladies and gentlemen. The drawings of Mrs. Monarch make her seem seven feet tall; the Major is useful only for brawny giants. The real thing, for the puzzled artist, keeps coming out larger than life, and he discovers "an innate preference for the represented subject over the real one: the defect of the real one was so apt to be a lack of representation."[16]

Another qualification concerning the realists' subject matter needs to be made. The common life and the ordinary

[15] Cf. C. D. Warner's "Modern Fiction," *Atlantic Monthly*, LI (April 1883), 464 ("photographic fidelity to nature"); William F. Thrall and Addison Hibbard's *A Handbook to Literature*, rev. and enl. by C. Hugh Holman (New York: Odyssey Press, 1960), p. 398 ("a one-to-one correspondence between the representation and the subject"); and Becker's "Realism: An Essay in Definition," p. 187 (the realist "keeps his eye on a statistical norm").

[16] *The Complete Tales of Henry James*, ed. Leon Edel (Philadelphia: J. B. Lippincott Co., 1962–64), VIII, 237.

characters on which the realists presumably depend are, upon close inspection, not so common and ordinary after all. Runaway slaves, millionaires, revolutionary suicides, and princesses (even democratic ones) are somewhat exceptional. And no important character in the fiction of Henry James can be lightly accused of being ordinary. Even Huck Finn is chosen as much for his unique social position as for his common humanity. "His liberties were totally unrestricted," said Mark Twain of Huck's prototype, Tom Blankenship of Hannibal. "He was the only really independent person— boy or man—in the community."[17] It is Huck's unique freedom which makes possible both the narrative structure of the book and its criticism of contemporary life, for his freedom gives him a distance from the community which makes critical perception possible (at least for the reader, through the point of view of the naïve narrator). Floating down the Mississippi on a raft has been seen as the great American experience. How many Americans have ever done it? The realists concern themselves with characters and events which are imaginatively representative of the common experience, even though the characters and events themselves may be somewhat out of the ordinary, outside the range of the statistical norm.

This point helps to explain the inappropriateness of Gordon Haight's witty rejoinder to Howells' praise of realistic subject matter in the "Editor's Study." In the most interesting American fiction, according to Howells,

nothing happens; that is, nobody murders or debauches anybody else; there is no arson or pillage of any sort; there is not a ghost, or a ravening beast, or a hair-breadth escape, or a shipwreck, or a monster of self-sacrifice, or a lady five thousand years old in the whole course of the story.[18]

Professor Haight comments:

[17] *The Autobiography of Mark Twain*, ed. Charles Neider (New York: Harper & Row, 1959), p. 73.
[18] *Harper's Monthly*, LXXXI (October 1890), 804.

Despite [Howells'] insistence that realism "prefers to avoid all manner of strange coincidences and dire catastrophes," his books abound in them. Three plots turn on train wrecks, three on fires; two characters are removed by brain fever, a number by sudden sickness; two commit suicide with poison; one hero is shot, another knocked down by a horsecar, and two others killed by locomotives.[19]

Realistic subject matter does have room for the exceptional, if it is the humanly exceptional (not the superhumanly or subhumanly exceptional, as in romantic and naturalistic writing). And it should be noted that Professor Haight's list is not quite analogous to Howells'. Fires, sicknesses, and train wrecks do happen, and with somewhat greater frequency than ladies five thousand years old. On Boston's Beacon Street in 1885, horsecars were more likely to be encountered than ghosts.

The subject matter of the realists is chosen from a middle ground. They reject the romance of the gutter as well as the romance of the ideal, a point not always clearly recognized. Charles Dudley Warner, writing in 1883, stated that "it is held to be artistic to look almost altogether upon the shady and the seamy side of life, giving to this view the name of 'realism'; to select the disagreeable, the vicious, the unwholesome." Warner concluded his catalogue of realistic subject matter with an exclamation that must have swayed the lambrequins in nineteenth-century parlors: "And this is called a picture of real life! Heavens!"[20] This common opinion concerning realism can be seen in the eleventh edition of the *Encyclopaedia Britannica*, which defined the realist as one who "describes ugly things and brings out de-

---

[19] "Realism Defined: William Dean Howells," *Literary History of the United States: History*, ed. R. E. Spiller *et al.*, 3d ed., rev. (New York: Macmillan Co., 1963), p. 894. Cf. Oscar W. Firkins, *William Dean Howells* (New York: Russell & Russell, 1963; orig. pub. 1924), pp. 230–232.

[20] "Modern Fiction," p. 471. It is difficult to reconcile this essay with Warner's collaboration with Mark Twain on *The Gilded Age*.

tails of an unsavoury sort,"[21] a definition epigrammatized by the acid pen of the devil's lexicographer, Ambrose Bierce: "Realism, n. The art of depicting nature as it is seen by toads."[22] George Becker, tracing realism well into the twentieth century, speaks of the subject matter of the "lower social levels," a view supported by Willard Thorp (realistic characters include "servants, laborers, privates in the army, immigrants, derelicts, the lonely ones, prostitutes, inhabitants of the urban slums and the worn-out farms") and James Colvert ("like the realists, Crane chose certain characteristic subjects and themes—slum life, war, prostitution, and alcoholism").[23]

Once again, however, we must separate realism from naturalism. The subject matter in the novels of the mid-1880's represents a *via media* between the castles of the romancers and the slums of the naturalists. The characters are essentially middle class, and the concerns of the novels are, for the most part, middle-class concerns. The realists open new areas of subject matter for fiction, but they do not open all areas. Overt sexuality, for example, was simply not possible in public American literature in the 1880's just as the bikini bathing suit was not possible on public American beaches in the nineteenth century. Even Mark Twain, who relished ribald tales and regretted that he had to modify for public printing the extravagant and gorgeous language of Jim Gillis of Jackass Gulch, spoke of fiction which poured from "Zola's sewer."[24] Howells' portraits of middle-class women and working girls—Marcia Hubbard, Zerrilla Mil-

---

[21] XXII, 941.

[22] *The Devil's Dictionary* (New York: Hill & Wang, 1957), p. 152. Orig. pub., in part, as *The Cynic's Word Book* in 1906.

[23] Becker, "Realism: An Essay in Definition," p. 191; Thorp, Introduction to *Great Short Works of American Realism* (New York: Harper & Row, 1968), p. xiv; Colvert, Introduction to *Great Short Works of Stephen Crane* (New York: Harper & Row, 1968), p. vii.

[24] *Mark Twain: Life as I Find It*, ed. Charles Neider (Garden City, N.Y.: Hanover House, 1961), p. 214. Private printing was another matter; witness *1601*.

lon Dewey, Statira Dudley, Amanda Grier—seem tame enough today, but they caused a momentous stir in their time. "How dare you speak out your beliefs as you do?" asked a letter to Howells, a letter not from Anthony Comstock or Agnes Repplier, but from the bold and masculine John William De Forest, a former combat commander of Company I of the Twelfth Connecticut Volunteers:

> You spare neither manhood nor womanhood, and especially not the latter, though it furnishes four-fifths of *our* novel-reading public. . . . Indeed I wonder in my admiration of your heroism, if you quite know what you are about. You are exposing to view the base metal and coarse clay of which nearly the whole American people is fabricated; and meantime this slag and half-baked mud is so conceited of itself, and so shop-girlishly touchy in its conceit![25]

Howells, of course, did not deal with sexuality or the lowest social levels, but he and the other realists helped to make these subjects possible for later writers. The realistic movement away from idealism, sentimentality, and romance is evolutionary: Statira Dudley and Zerrilla Dewey are a step toward Crane's Maggie and Dreiser's Carrie. The overtones of Lesbianism in *The Bostonians* are muted but unmistakable.[26] Howells and James, while not dealing directly with sex, do shatter the idealistic (yet hypocritical) nineteenth-century feminine pedestal and open up the entire question of the status of women and their relations with men. Romantic novelist Amelia Barr criticized the realists for depicting girls who were not "nice," girls who were frank, highhanded, freethinking, and contemptuous of

[25] James F. Light, *John William De Forest* (New York: Twayne Publishers, 1965), p. 166. De Forest himself had difficulty in finding publishers for his candid fiction.

[26] James once complained that "we grope in darkness—that airless gloom of false delicacy in which the light of life quite goes out" ("The Novel of Dialect; W. D. Howells," *Literature* [9 July 1898]; quoted in *Henry James: The American Essays*, ed. Leon Edel [New York: Vintage Books, 1956], p. 252).

authority, girls who rode bicycles, played tennis, and rowed boats—"altogether in accord with an epoch that travels . . . sixty miles an hour."[27] Charles Dudley Warner also condemned the realists for their portraits of "the silly and weak-minded woman, the fast and slangy girl, the *intrigante* and the 'shady.' "[28] It must have distressed Warner to find that the issue of the *Atlantic* which carried his condemnation had, as its leading piece, James' three-act dramatic version of *Daisy Miller*.

This context of nineteenth-century thought and the realists' dynamic innovations have been ignored by the short-sighted critics who condemn Howells and James (and Mark Twain, to a lesser extent) for the restricted range of their subject matter. It is the realists' extension of the subject matter previously available to fiction that has opened the door to modern literature (a door which, in recent decades, has been taken off its hinges). Such critics as Van Wyck Brooks, H. L. Mencken, Sinclair Lewis, V. L. Parrington, Granville Hicks, Maxwell Geismar, and Leslie Fiedler are suffering from the historical fallacy of judging the past by the present—a process which tends effectively to obscure both past and present.[29]

[27] "The Modern Novel," *North American Review*, CLIX (November 1894), 598. Mrs. Barr sighed for those good old-fashioned girls "who thought their parents infallible and who were reverent church-women—the girls who were so shrinkingly modest, and yet so brave in great emergencies—the girls who were so fully accomplished and so beautiful, and who yet had no higher ambition than to be the dearly loved wife of a noble-hearted man and the good house-mother of happy children."

[28] LI (April 1883), 471.

[29] These opinions are by no means limited to the more outspoken (if not outrageous) critics. Professor Samuel Chew, for example, is convinced that James' restricted subject matter has doomed his literary reputation: "With the disappearance of his 'world' the books . . . are likely to become, save in the estimation of a small and diminishing band of devotees, mere documents in the history of a phase of European sensibility almost as remote from today's actualities as is the *Carte du Tendre*" (in *A Literary History of England*, ed.

"Humor," said Mark Twain, "must not professedly teach and it must not professedly preach, but it must do both if it would live forever."[30] Howells and James would agree, and would expand the statement from humor to all fiction, for the ethical content of realistic novels is so essential that it demands a place as an integral part of the definition of realism. The morality of realism has not always been recognized. Nineteenth-century critics attacked *The Rise of Silas Lapham* as "a book whose moral tone was so unpleasantly, so hopelessly bad."[31] The Concord Library Committee stumbled into fame by calling *Adventures of Huckleberry Finn* "rough, coarse, and inelegant . . . the veriest trash" and banning the book from the library's refined, elegant, and grammatical shelves. The Library Committee was not, as is sometimes thought, simply another isolated manifestation of Massachusetts contrariness. The committee's opinion was apparently a majority one, and was seconded by such diverse publications as the *Arkansaw Traveler* ("Mark Twain's latest book . . . is vulgar and coarse") and the Springfield *Republican* (The "moral level [of Twain's books]

ethical

A. C. Baugh [New York: Appleton-Century-Crofts, 1948], p. 1551). That small band of devotees seems to consist of avid book buyers, for there are currently one hundred thirty-four volumes and collections of James' works in print, according to Bowker's *Books in Print* (1967). The charges of avoiding experience which have been leveled against James blatantly ignore *The Bostonians* and *The Princess Casamassima.* Moreover, they ignore James' entire commitment to experience, summarized by his prefatory highlighting of the essence of *The Ambassadors*: "Live all you can; it's a mistake not to." And it is James who has drawn the classic portrait of the man who refused experience—John Marcher in "The Beast in the Jungle." The fact that James uses a Hemingway metaphor of hairy-chested experience—the final, fatal spring of the hideous beast—to capture Marcher's realization of his tragedy of nothingness, well expresses the depth of James' irony and his art.

[30] *Autobiography*, ed. Neider, p. 298. Characteristically, Mark Twain goes on to deflate his own rhetoric: "By forever, I mean thirty years."

[31] "Novel-Writing as a Science," *Catholic World*, LXII (November 1885), 279.

is low, and their perusal can not be anything less than harmful").[32]

Other critics questioned the moral vision of the realists, but on different grounds. Charles F. Richardson accused realistic writing of being amoral, rather than immoral: "For the purpose of the present study it may be sufficient to say that it [realism] stands without, not within; gives no evidence of personal sympathy; seldom indulges in reflections upon the narrative it offers; leaves the reader to draw his own conclusions concerning right, wrong, progress, and remedy."[33] Richardson's charge of amorality has been repeated by some twentieth-century critics, who are often more concerned with aesthetics than with ethics. The realist's illusion of "objectivity"[34] has led some readers to suppose that the realist "served no interest and adhered to no philosophy of social action." Or, if the realist is unable to maintain his uncommitted "objectivity," he arrives at "the delicate point at which realism ends and overt social criticism begins."[35] The charge of amorality has also been made against Henry James, on somewhat different grounds. James, it is often said, sacrifices morality on the all-consuming altar of his Art. He has substituted "psychological for ethical measurements of good and evil,"[36] although it is by no means clear what the difference is.

In spite of these criticisms, perceptive readers have long been aware of the fundamental moral orientation of Amer-

[32] Arthur L. Vogelback, "The Publication and Reception of *Huckleberry Finn* in America," *American Literature*, XI (November 1939), 269–271.

[33] *American Literature: 1607–1885* (New York: G. P. Putnam's Sons, 1888), II, 431–432. The leader of the realistic school was Henry James, according to Richardson. Mark Twain is almost totally ignored in the two-volume study, and if Richardson read *Huckleberry Finn*, he didn't admit it.

[34] Discussed above, pp. 33–35.

[35] Becker, "Realism: An Essay in Definition," p. 188.

[36] Robert E. Spiller, *The Cycle of American Literature* (New York: New American Library, 1957), p. 135.

ican realism. Joel Chandler Harris immediately recognized that "there is not in our fictive literature a more wholesome book than 'Huckleberry Finn.' . . . We are taught [by it] the lesson of honesty, justice, and mercy."[37] Unlike many contemporary critics, Harris realized that the ethical force of *Huckleberry Finn* and the other realistic novels was not based upon external spiritual forces but upon the confrontation of human beings in a humanly created social environment. The realists' morality is intrinsic, integral, relativistic; it arises from the characters and the narrative action, rather than being superimposed upon them. Significant fiction has always been ethical, and the realists come to rather conventional conclusions about the qualities men must have in dealing with each other—honesty, justice, mercy, love. What is new in 1885 is that these qualities are no longer sought in an external, transcendental system of values. Realistic protagonists are forced to work out their own codes of behavior, appropriate to their individual circumstances.

Howells, James, and Mark Twain do not professedly teach or preach. They do not step to the front of the stage and tell the reader how to interpret their puppets. On the other hand, the realists do not ignore interpretation. Since the moral arises from the fabric of the fictional experience, interpretation is built into the narrative. The reader makes the interpretation for himself, but if he is a careful reader he makes the interpretation that the author desires. The reader's freedom to choose, like the realist's "objectivity," is largely an illusion.

Alfred Kazin has remarked that Howells' morality, like Tolstoy's, meant "the relation of man to his society."[38] The observation is valid for all the realists, and the fiction of the mid-1880's explores the relations between man and society in a variety of ways. *Adventures of Huckleberry Finn* con-

[37] *Critic*, VII (28 November 1885), 253. Quoted by Vogelback, "Publication of *Huckleberry Finn*," p. 271.

[38] *On Native Grounds* (Garden City, N.Y.: Doubleday & Co., 1956), p. viii.

tains a double pattern: the condemnation of religious, political, and social opinions which are held by fools and
exploited by knaves and the affirmation of brotherhood
through the relation of Huck and Jim. Huck faces a dilemma
common in realistic fiction. When he finds that Jim has been
sold back into slavery by the King, Huck is forced to decide
between a fixed code of public morality and an inner ethical
impulse—a conflict which he resolves at the climax of *Huckleberry Finn*:

I was a trembling, because I'd got to decide, forever, betwixt two
things, and I knowed it. I studied a minute, sort of holding my
breath, and then says to myself:
"All right, then, I'll *go* to hell."[39]

Huck chooses hell and humanity; his sound heart triumphs
over the conscience which has been deformed by a morally
corrupt society.[40]

Huck's sound heart can be heard beating in another of
Mark Twain's works published in 1885, "The Private History of a Campaign That Failed," which tells of Sam Clemens' two-week fling at soldiering in the summer of 1861. Like
most of Twain's autobiographical writings, the "Campaign"
has only a casual acquaintance with historical accuracy; but
whether fact or fiction, the central episode of the piece, and
Twain's treatment of it, is revealing. The holiday spirit of
the boys in Twain's company is broken when, dazed with
fear, they shoot an unarmed stranger who happens by their
camp at night. The death preys on young Clemens:

[39] *Adventures of Huckleberry Finn* (New York: Charles L. Webster
& Co., 1885), p. 272.

[40] Twain once referred to *Huckleberry Finn* as "a book of mine
where a sound heart & a deformed conscience come into collision
& conscience suffers defeat" (Notebook no. 28a [I], TS, p. 35 [1895],
Mark Twain Papers, University of California Library, Berkeley);
quoted in *Adventures of Huckleberry Finn*, ed. Henry Nash Smith
(Boston: Houghton Mifflin Co., 1958), p. xvi. Huck's decision is totally
serious, but it suggests an idea that runs through much of Mark
Twain's lighter work: Heaven for climate; hell for society.

I could not get rid of it. I could not drive it away, the taking of that unoffending life seemed such a wanton thing. And it seemed an epitome of war; that all war must be just that—the killing of strangers against whom you feel no personal animosity; strangers whom, in other circumstances, you would help if you found them in trouble, and who would help you if you needed it.[41]

This taste of war added a new activity to Twain's growing list of publicly sanctioned insanities and immoralities and ended his brief experience as a Confederate irregular. He soon lit out for the Territory with his brother Orion.

Like Huck Finn, Silas Lapham struggles with a difficult and lonely moral decision for which he has no precedent, and, like Huck, he wins a moral victory. Lapham's final rise is an ethical one, climaxed when he refuses to sell his western milling property, which he knows to be of little value, to English buyers. This decision is made difficult by Lapham's cascading series of financial disasters and more difficult by the apparent dishonesty of the Englishmen, who represent "rich and charitable" investors who will not feel the loss of the money which could save Lapham. A further loophole is provided by Colonel Lapham's ex-partner Rogers, who offers to serve as a middleman in the purchase and thus relieve Lapham of any legal responsibility. He is tempted and confused, but Lapham resists the offer until it is no longer feasible. Morally strengthened by this victory of hesitation, he is then easily able to refuse to sell the paint works in Vermont to a New York agent who is unaware of the declining market value of Lapham's mineral paint. Silas Lapham's fall from business, from wealth, and from Beacon Street is complete.

[41] *Century Magazine*, XXXI (December 1885), p. 203. In 1909 Thomas Hardy expressed the same thought in "The Man He Killed," a poem based upon a remarkably similar dramatic situation:

"Yes; quaint and curious war is!
You shoot a fellow down
You'd treat if met where any bar is,
Or help to half-a-crown."

(Reprinted with permission of The Macmillan Company from *Collected Poems* by Thomas Hardy, p. 269. Copyright 1925 by The Macmillan Company.)

He retires to his Vermont farm, and taking his poverty with better grace than his success, closes his story with a laconic but sincere testimony to morality: "I don't know as I should always say it paid; but if I done it, and the thing was to do over again, right in the same way, I guess I should have to do it."[42]

Howells' two other novels in the period also demonstrate ethical concerns. In *Indian Summer* Theodore Colville achieves an amiable moral victory over his illusions of youth and is conventionally rewarded with the hand of Mrs. Bowen, a widow who, like Colville, is enjoying the agreeable weather in the afternoon of life. But underneath the placid surface and the pleasant ironies of *Indian Summer* is a tough-minded attack on conventional romantic notions and heroic self-sacrifice, favorite Howellsian targets. Colville's dishonest dream of himself lies shattered along the banks of the Arno, just as that corrupt steamboat, the *Walter Scott*, is wrecked along the Mississippi in *Huckleberry Finn*.

In *The Minister's Charge; or, The Apprenticeship of Lemuel Barker* Howells develops another moral theme which he uses for the rest of his career—complicity.[43] The Reverend David Sewell discovers that he is responsible for Lemuel Barker, a Willoughby Pastures boy who is accidentally introduced to the complexities of Boston life by Sewell. Barker himself learns that he is responsible for Statira Dudley, a working girl whom he gradually transcends in his social rise. All of the proper Bostonians learn that they cannot insulate themselves from the swindlers on the Common, the line-up at the city police station, and the indigent tramps at the Wayfarers' Lodge. And the reader is enlightened by a series of

[42] *The Rise of Silas Lapham, Century Magazine*, XXX (August 1885), 526.

[43] The word "complicity" has an almost exclusively negative meaning in the twentieth century, probably because of its use in legal terminology and its guilt-by-association relationship to "accomplice." *Webster's New World Dictionary* gives "partnership in wrongdoing." Howells, of course, with an eye to the Latin root ("weave together"), means partnership in mankind.

discussions on complicity which culminate in Howells' re-capitulation of Sewell's sermon:

No one for good or for evil, for sorrow or joy, for sickness or health, stood apart from his fellows, but each was bound to the highest and the lowest by ties that centered in the hand of God. No man, he said, sinned or suffered to himself alone; his error and his pain darkened and afflicted men who never heard of his name. If a community was corrupt, if an age was immoral, it was not because of the vicious, but the virtuous who fancied themselves indifferent spectators.[44]

Howells' three novels in the mid-1880's not only show a concern for ethics, they also demonstrate a pattern of moral development, a pattern which accurately reflects Howells' continually deepening thought. *Indian Summer*, written first, contains the lesson that we must live honestly with ourselves. *Silas Lapham* extends the point, for Lapham discovers that honesty to self demands honesty to others. And the reader of *The Minister's Charge* learns the fundamental Christian doctrine that honesty is not enough, that we must involve ourselves with mankind. The Reverend Mr. Sewell comes to realize, somewhat to his surprise, that even a Boston minister is a piece of the continent, a part of the main.

In the closing pages of *Silas Lapham*, Mr. Sewell (one of several peripatetic characters who appear in different Howells novels) observes that "we can trace the operation of evil in the physical world . . . but I'm more and more puzzled about it in the moral world. There its course is often so very obscure. . . ." Henry James would thoroughly agree, for, characteristically, the morality of his novels is less obvious than that of Howells, but no less central to his artistic purpose. *The Bostonians* is a novel without a hero, and emphatically a novel without a heroine. There is no moral mouthpiece, no center of reference, for Basil Ransom

[44] *The Minister's Charge, Century Magazine*, XXXIII (December 1886), 191. Privately, out of his pulpit, Sewell puts his doctrine more simply: "Everybody seems to be tangled up with everybody else" (p. 191).

is no more "right" than the Bostonians to whom he is a foil. The moral, as usual for James, must be drawn by inference, by implication—ultimately, by character. With the exception of Verena Tarrant, the malleable prize, all of the characters, whether reformers or reactionaries, Northerners or Southerners, are motivated by selfishness. The main conflict, that of Basil and Olive over Verena, is one of will rather than of love, and each wants her for his own satisfaction. Selah Tarrant, like Hollingsworth, his spiritual ancestor in Hawthorne's *Blithedale Romance*, is a "moralist without moral sense,"[45] who rents his daughter to Olive on a yearly basis. The reform movement itself, with its sacrifices and its martyrdoms, is seen as an exercise in ego. The entire group is transfixed on the shrill point of Olive's despairing concern for herself: "I shall see nothing but shame and ruin!" The novel's coda is provided, ironically, by self-seeking Mrs. Tarrant: "It's the most horrible, wicked, immoral selfishness I ever heard in my life!"[46]

In *The Princess Casamassima* the reformers are changed to revolutionaries, and shame and ruin of a different sort stalk the novel's anguished protagonist, Hyacinth Robinson. Intellectually and emotionally torn, Hyacinth cannot carry out his mysterious assignment. His revolutionary convictions are not strong enough to overcome his morality, and unable to assassinate the duke, Hyacinth shoots himself instead, through the heart.

In spite of the variety of these six works, their underlying moral orientation is clear. In addition, they have many ethical points in common. Both *Indian Summer* and *The Bostonians* show that self-sacrifice is often self-aggrandizement. Complicity is the official lesson of *The Minister's Charge*, but it applies as well to *Huckleberry Finn*. James' portraits of selfishness are reverse images of the Howellsian doctrine of complicity, for the preoccupation with self precludes involvement with others. Howells, James, and

---

[45] *Century Magazine*, XXIX (April 1885), 907.
[46] *Ibid.*, XXXI (January 1886), 341; XXXI (February 1886), 597.

Mark Twain agree that we fully become human beings only when we escape the prison of the ego. This affirmation of basic human values should exculpate the realists from charges of immorality and amorality, although such moral themes are not new, by any means. Huck's raft was preceded by a good many vessels, the *Pequod* among them, for the lesson of the monkey-rope is as applicable to Huck and Jim as it is to Ishmael and Queequeg, even though Twain, characteristically, refuses to editorialize or overtly symbolize the relationship. What the realists contribute in their discussion of human values is the emphasis on the complexity of moral choice and the necessity of individual decision in a human context, unassisted by external spiritual forces. And these values are dramatized rather than sermonized in the novels of the mid-1880's (with the minor exception of the sermons of the Reverend Mr. Sewell, which are, after all, occupationally justified), for the realist refuses to "stand about in his scene, talking it over with his hands in his pockets, interrupting the action, and spoiling the illusion."[47]

The relation of moral content to dramatization, theme to technique, leads us to the fourth significant category which can be used to define American realism in the 1880's— style. Realistic style is the vehicle which carries realistic philosophy, subject matter, and morality. It is the link between the theory and its artistic application, between the idea and the narrative, which converts concepts into patterns of words, paragraphs, and chapters.

There is a curious irony concerning discussions of realistic style. In the wake of the New Criticism, scholars are virtually unanimous in their statements of the significance of the realists' technique. There is an impressive chorus of critical comment which sings the importance of style in realism. Ian Watt differentiates between "realism of assessment"

[47] "Editor's Study," *Harper's Monthly*, LXXIX (November 1889), 967.

and "realism of presentation" and states that "the novel's realism does not reside in the kind of life it presents, but in the way it presents it."[48] Marcus Cunliffe notes that "with Mark Twain, *content*—like Western life—had a mongrel incongruity; but *form* began the lineage that has led to Hemingway."[49] Gordon Haight claims that "realism is determined less by choice of material than by intention and method of treatment."[50] Similar views are held by Wallace Stegner ("realism of *method*"), H. Wayne Morgan ("By realism, I mean simply a literary technique"), Lars Åhnebrink ("a manner and method of composition"), L. W. Smith ("Realism is willing to remain a literary method"), James D. Hart ("Realistic technique continues to be dominant"), and George Becker ("The perennial phase . . . is what may be called realism of method").

Having sung these brief introductory anthems, the voices stop. For many critics, the mere statement that style is an important part of realism is enough, and they fail to discuss what that style is and how it operates. Others go further, and discuss objective presentation, realistic details, and the vernacular, but they do not take full advantage of realistic technique as a useful handle for definition.[51] The following

[48] *The Rise of the Novel* (Berkeley, Calif.: University of California Press, 1962), pp. 11, 290–291.

[49] *The Literature of the United States* (Baltimore: Penguin Books, 1954), p. 169.

[50] "Realism Defined: William Dean Howells," *Literary History of the U. S.: History*, p. 894.

[51] There is as little critical agreement about the meaning of the word "style" (and such terms as form, technique, structure, and texture) as there is concerning realism. For the purposes of this discussion and the chapters to follow, style is synonymous with form and technique. It is used in the broad sense defined by Mark Schorer in his discussion of technique: "Modern criticism has shown us that to speak of content as such is not to speak of art at all, but of experience; and that it is only when we speak of the *achieved* content, the form, the work of art as a work of art, that we speak as critics. The difference between content, or experience, and achieved content, or art, is technique. When we speak of technique, then, we speak of

chapters will consider in detail the main aspects of nineteenth-century American realistic style—its antiomniscient point of view, its complexity and ambiguity, its concern with character, and its tendency to be imagistic rather than symbolic. Such emphasis on technique is, in many respects, the best introduction to realistic fiction, for the realists strongly believed in (and skillfully practiced) the concept of organic form, the appropriateness of technique to subject. Thus style can be a useful key in unlocking the novels and in analyzing the similarities and differences between realism and other kinds of writing.

Recent decades have too often seen the exploitation of the stylistic approach and its degeneration into metaphor mongering and syntax torture, but such excesses do not negate the method. A consideration of technique, like every critical approach, is justified only if it leads to a deeper understanding of the work at hand. For the fiction of the mid-1880's, stylistic analysis is useful both in the consideration of individual works and in defining the movement as a whole, since style is ultimately the means of embodying the realistic sensibility in literary works of art. From this point on, then, our purpose, as Milton observed over three centuries ago, will be "not to make verbal curiosities the end, that were a toylsom vanity, but to be an interpreter & relater of the best and sagest things."[52]

---

nearly everything. For technique is the means by which the writer's experience, which is his subject matter, compels him to attend to it; technique is the only means he has of discovering, exploring, developing his subject, of conveying its meaning, and, finally, of evaluating it. . . . In this sense, everything is technique which is not the lump of experience itself" ("Technique as Discovery," *Hudson Review*, I [Spring 1948], 67, 69). Cf. M. H. Abrams: "Style . . . is *how* a speaker or writer says whatever he says" (*A Glossary of Literary Terms* [New York: Holt, Rinehart & Winston, 1957], p. 91).

[52] *The Reason of Church-Government Urg'd against Prelaty* (1641), *The Works of John Milton* (New York: Columbia University Press, 1931), III, pt. 1, 236.

THE STYLE OF
AMERICAN REALISM

CHAPTER V

A VANISHING INSTINCT
The Rejection of Omniscience

THE American generation born in the late 1830's and early 1840's—that of Howells, James, and Mark Twain—had another member who, in many respects, wrote the autobiography of his age. The formalities of Henry Adams' education contrast sharply with the occasional and desultory classroom experiences of Howells, James, and Twain, but his *Education of Henry Adams* portrays the intellectual complexities faced by an entire generation. Adams' discussion of religion and its disappearance during his teen-age years effectively summarizes the theological dilemma in the middle and late nineteenth century:

Of all the conditions of his youth which afterwards puzzled the grown-up man, this disappearance of religion puzzled him most. The boy went to church twice every Sunday; he was taught to read his Bible, and he learned religious poetry by heart; he believed in a mild deism; he prayed; he went through all the forms; but neither to him nor to his brothers or sisters was religion real. Even the mild discipline of the Unitarian Church was so irksome that they all threw it off at the first possible moment, and never afterwards entered a church. The religious instinct had vanished, and could not be revived.[1]

The disappearance of the religious instinct was both a result and a cause—a result of the profound scientific and philosophical upheavals occurring in the middle of the nineteenth century (Adams mentions Darwin and Comte as the

---

[1] *The Education of Henry Adams* (Boston: Houghton Mifflin Co., 1961; priv. pr. 1907, posthumously pub. 1918), p. 34.

most important influences on the age) and a cause of further intellectual and cultural dislocation. This dislocation was not a private problem, as an Adams could half-seriously believe, but a public issue that plagued most of the educated population in late nineteenth-century America. James Russell Lowell versified the matter in 1888:

> Men feel old systems cracking under 'em;
> Life saddens to a mere conundrum
> Which once Religion solved, but she
> Has lost—has Science found?—the key.[2]

The realists did not have the advantages, ambiguous as they were to Henry Adams, of the mild Unitarian forms. Howells, James, and Twain, all sons of freethinking fathers, were theologically reared in Swedenborgianism, Sweden-

---

[2] "Credidimus Jovem Regnare," *The Writings of James Russell Lowell* (Boston: Houghton, Mifflin & Co., 1897), XI, 234. Lowell's point, but not his poetry, suggests Donne's famous lament that

> New Philosophy calls all in doubt,
> The Element of fire is quite put out;
> The Sun is lost, and th'earth, and no mans wit
> Can well direct him where to looke for it.

("An Anatomie of the World: The First Anniversary," *The Poems of John Donne*, ed. Herbert Grierson [Oxford: Oxford University Press, 1912], I, 237.)

There is a fruitful analogy between these *fin de siècle* expressions. The closing years of both the sixteenth and nineteenth centuries saw severe intellectual disturbances which gave rise to skepticism and often pessimism. Both periods witnessed the delayed impact of new scientific ideas which had their roots earlier in the century (Copernicus published "De Revolutionibus" in 1543; Darwin first outlined his doctrine of natural selection in 1844). At the end of the sixteenth century the principles of order in God's world seemed lost. At the end of the nineteenth century God himself seemed lost, and his creative *fiat*, his divine son, his very existence, were all called into question. Conservatives in both periods were dismayed, scientists such as Lord Bacon and T. H. Huxley were generally optimistic, and writers reflected these profound and complex disturbances in new literary styles, which, in both periods, rejected the romanticism of the past and turned to contemporary subject matter, satire, and colloquial rhythms.

borgian eclecticism, and Mississippi miscellany, respectively. All became agnostics; and the looseness of the term is quite appropriate because the realists, like many creative writers, were not rigid or even systematic in their theology and philosophy. Nevertheless, their books abundantly demonstrate the disappearance of the religious instinct, a phenomenon uniformly illustrated in the biographies. Dixon Wecter writes of Mark Twain following the skeptic's road blazed by his father, "a lonely road, because agnosticism was feared as much as Romanism by the society in which [he] grew up."[3] Howells mentions Twain's "first fine flush of . . . agnosticism" and summarizes the religious beliefs of his friend by stating that Mark never held "anything like faith in the Christian theology, or in the notion of life after death, or in a conscious divinity."[4] Howells, himself, it is clear, "never became, in the ordinary churchly sense, a Christian. Theologically, metaphysically, intellectually, even perhaps spiritually, he remained an agnostic. . . . As a realist he was deprived of the romantic's faith in the sublimity of his ego, and as an agnostic deprived of the believer's faith in the support of the cosmos."[5] Churchgoing

[3] *Sam Clemens of Hannibal* (Boston: Houghton Mifflin Co., 1961), p. 231. Young Sam attended a Methodist and then a Presbyterian Sunday School, as his mother's whims changed; his father avoided churches altogether. His brother Orion tried, in addition to Methodism and Presbyterianism, Baptism, Universalism, and heresy. Mark said of him that "in light matters—matters of small consequence, like religion and politics and such things—he never acquired a conviction that could survive a disapproving remark from a cat" (*Autobiography*, ed. Charles Neider [New York: Harper & Row, 1959], p. 93). The *Autobiography*, especially chapter 49, spells out Twain's religious convictions with clarity: "I have long ago lost my belief in immortality—also my interest in it" (p. 271).

[4] *My Mark Twain* (New York: Harper & Bros., 1910), pp. 31–32.

[5] Edwin H. Cady, *The Realist at War* (Syracuse: Syracuse University Press, 1958), p. 9. Everett Carter disagrees to some extent, stating (on rather slim intuitive evidence) that Howells believed in a "kind of idealistic materialism" (*Howells and the Age of Realism* [Philadelphia: J. B. Lippincott Co., 1954], p. 27). See also Hannah Graham

for Henry James, when he occasionally and randomly went, "was essentially a participation in a social phenomenon rather than a religious experience."[6]

The relation between an author's religion and his writing, between his philosophy and his imagination, is a matter of complexity and even mystery. The relation is rarely simple or direct, and its circuitous path may be difficult to follow, even for the writer himself. Some writers—the American naturalists furnish excellent examples—seem to be at internal cross-purposes, their theories of fiction conflicting with their practice. Equally difficult is the relation of an author's ideas to his cultural environment, a relation that is so complex and often so casual that it may be impossible to reconstruct in anything other than the most general terms. Quoting Turgenev, Henry James noted the impossibility of ever knowing "the origin of one's wind-blown germs. . . . We have to go too far back, too far behind, to say. Isn't it all we can say that they come from every quarter of heaven . . . floated into our minds by the current of life.'"[7] Proving this theory, James found his germ for *The Princess Casamassima* not in the pages of *Das Kapital*, but in the streets of London.

Without attempting to oversimplify, without claiming a one-to-one relationship between the realists' agnosticism and their aesthetics, it seems clear that somehow, in whatever complicated manner, there is an important relationship between the realists' loss of the religious instinct and their wholehearted commitment to antiomniscience in fiction. Without trying to analyze that relationship, we can discuss its fruits in what is perhaps the most significant aspect of realistic style—point of view.

Belcher, "Howells's Opinions on the Religious Conflicts of His Age as Exhibited in Magazine Articles," *American Literature*, XV (November 1943), 262–278.

[6] Leon Edel, *Henry James: The Untried Years, 1843–1870* (Philadelphia: J. B. Lippincott Co., 1953), p. 111.

[7] Preface to *The Portrait of a Lady*, in *The Art of the Novel*, ed. R. P. Blackmur (New York: Charles Scribner's Sons, 1934), p. 43.

Point of view in a work of fiction controls the way in which the material is presented to the reader. It is commonly discussed in either of two ways: *who* is telling the story to the reader (a major character, a minor character, the author, the author concealed behind a screen of anonymity) or *what* is being told (narrative action, description, evaluation). If these two approaches are grouped together, three general possibilities emerge: (1) the dramatic presentation of a scene at which the reader presumedly is present and over-hears the characters speak ("scene," in James' term); (2) the description of scene or action at second hand—a résumé, which can be made by a character or in the author-narrator's third-person voice ("picture" according to James and Percy Lubbock); (3) comment or evaluation upon the story, or any other matter, which again can be made either through a character or by the author-narrator.[8]

These three modes of presentation are rarely pure or un-mixed. Many "scenes" are glued together with "pictures," and both scenes and pictures often contain evaluation. *The*

---

[8] The term "author-narrator" seems useful to distinguish the voice of the author from that of a character-narrator (such as Huck), who may present part or all of a story. The term is also preferable to "author," since the author may be a man of many attitudes, many books, many poses. "Author-narrator," then, means the author as he chooses to represent himself while telling the story under con-sideration, a representation that may range from an impersonal third-person pose to the stage managership of Fielding, Trollope, and Thackeray. Wayne Booth, in *The Rhetoric of Fiction* (Chicago: University of Chicago Press, 1961), suggests "implied author" for the same concept (p. 151). Booth uses "scene," "summary," and "com-mentary" (pp. 154–155) for the three types of narration discussed above, a division contested by Wellek and Warren (*Theory of Literature*, 3d ed. [New York: Harcourt, Brace & World, 1962], pp. 223–224), who make what seems to be an unnecessary differentia-tion between "picture" and "summary." More elaborate distinctions are made by Norman Friedman, "Point of View in Fiction: The De-velopment of a Critical Concept," *PMLA*, LXX (December 1955), 1160–1184; and Bertil Romberg, *Studies in the Narrative Technique of the First-Person Novel* (Stockholm: Almqvist & Wiksell, 1962).

Rise of Silas Lapham is justly celebrated for its dramatic, scenic opening, but close investigation reveals a certain amount of residual description and evaluation. " 'Take your time,' said Bartley, with the ease he instantly felt." The effect of Bartley's remark is reinforced by the author-narrator's evaluation of what it indicates about the journalist's too-casual attitude. " 'There!' Lapham pounded with his great hairy fist on the envelope he had been addressing." The "great hairy fist," even the use of "pounded" rather than pressed, begins a series of judgments on Lapham, and the reader will not be surprised, a few chapters hence, to find Silas putting his great hairy foot in his mouth.

Like many analytical terms, these modes of presentation—scene, picture, evaluation—are oversimplified; but they are useful in discussing point of view, and they provide a basis for considering realistic style. The realists put great emphasis upon scenic presentation, de-emphasizing authorial comment and evaluation. The personality of the author as an editorial commentator, a loquacious puppeteer, is largely removed. The realists object to the omniscient author who gives himself away by entering his fiction and destroying the illusion, an objection forcefully made by James in "The Art of Fiction":

Certain accomplished novelists have a habit of giving themselves away which must often bring tears to the eyes of people who take their fiction seriously. I was lately struck, in reading over many pages of Anthony Trollope, with his want of discretion in this particular. In a digression, a parenthesis or an aside, he concedes to the reader that he and this trusting friend are only "making believe." He admits that the events he narrates have not really happened, and that he can give his narrative any turn the reader may like best. Such a betrayal of a sacred office seems to me, I confess, a terrible crime.[9]

The realists, of course, cannot have all "scene," and they use a good deal of "picture," often in the third-person voice

[9] "The Art of Fiction," *Longman's Magazine*, IV (September 1884), 504.

of the author-narrator. Here, however, the realists tend to depart from traditional narrative technique by presenting (as much as possible) the picture as seen through the filter of the consciousness of a particular character. The unfiltered presence of the author-narrator, as Mark Twain noted in a discussion of *The Last of the Mohicans*, tends to distract the reader. Twain analyzed one of Cooper's Indian dinner parties of uncooked venison. After killing a fawn, one of the Indians was "employed, in common with his fellows, in gorging himself with this digestible sustenance. Magua alone sat apart, without participating in the revolting meal." Who is it, asks Twain, that is revolted by the meal? Surely not Magua, since he is an Indian and likes raw meat. It is Cooper who is revolted, and we are not interested in his opinion.[10]

In his Preface to *The American*, James summarized the realists' attempt to keep the narrative focus on the individual character: "It is *his* vision, *his* conception, *his* interpretation: at the window of his . . . consciousness we are seated. . . . He therefore supremely matters; all the rest matters only as he feels it, treats it, meets it."[11] Thus the realists' antiomniscience results in a twofold attempt to remove the external presence of the author through dramatic representation and through the effort to present description and summary, even when it is written in the third person (traditionally the territory of the omniscient author), from the angle of vision of the characters.

Before we consider specifically the realistic point of view in the fiction of the mid-1880's, it should be noted that there is no need to refute those embarrassing allies of the

[10] "Fenimore Cooper's Further Literary Offenses," ed. Bernard De Voto, *New England Quarterly*, XIX (September 1946), 293, 297.

[11] *The Art of the Novel*, p. 37. Another realist, J. W. De Forest, put it more bluntly: "I am not trying to show how things really were, but only how the Colonel looked at them" (*Miss Ravenel's Conversion from Secession to Loyalty*, ed. Gordon S. Haight [New York: Holt, Rinehart & Winston, 1955; orig. pub. 1867], p. 100).

realistic method who, having drunk the strong wine of anti-omniscience, have become intoxicated. Ford Madox Ford, Percy Lubbock, and many others (including countless well-meaning teachers of composition) would have us believe that the antiomniscient way is the only way, that "showing" is always superior to "telling." These dragons have been neatly speared by Wayne Booth in *The Rhetoric of Fiction*. The antiomniscient way is, of course, not totally nonomniscient; it rarely even attempts to preserve the illusion of total non-omniscience. And it is not necessarily superior to any other method. Meaningful omniscient editorializing is obviously preferable to poorly written scenes. Hemingway's "The Killers," that apotheosis of antiomniscience in which the author carefully covers his tracks, is, after all, no more successful as a literary work of art than Thackeray's *Vanity Fair*, in which the author invites himself to take tea and conversation with the reader. The antiomniscient method, however, does have certain advantages which the realists found particularly useful.

Howells, James, and Mark Twain shared the instinct for the antiomniscient point of view, but it took many forms in the varieties of their artistic experience. The most striking case is *Adventures of Huckleberry Finn*. Ever since *Century* reviewer Thomas S. Perry noted the success of Twain's use of the "autobiographical form" in 1885, critics have praised the first-person point of view of *Huckleberry Finn*.[12] Much of the novel is dramatic, although Perry exaggerated when he claimed that "every scene is given, not described." There

[12] *Century Magazine*, XXX (May 1885), 171–172. The literature on the style of *Huckleberry Finn* would fill a small steamboat. A profitable beginning can be made with two key articles: Leo Marx, "The Pilot and the Passenger: Landscape Conventions and the Style of *Huckleberry Finn*," *American Literature*, XXVIII (May 1956), 129–146; and John C. Gerber, "The Relation between Point of View and Style in the Works of Mark Twain," *Style in Prose Fiction: English Institute Essays, 1958*, ed. Harold C. Martin (New York: Columbia University Press, 1959), pp. 142–171.

are also descriptions, summaries, and evaluations; but all, of course, are given from Huck's angle of vision and, most importantly, in his language. Huck's point of view starts with the first sentence ("You don't know about me, without you have read a book by the name of 'The Adventures of Tom Sawyer,' but that ain't no matter") and is consistently maintained to the last page, which Huck signs like a letter ("The end. Yours truly, Huck Finn"). This accounts for much of the success of the book—its unity (a result of Huck's character, rather than plot), its freshness (a joint product of Huck's unfettered judgments and the vernacular which embodies them), and its integrity (achieved through the harmony of style and content).

Mark Twain has constructed all of the novel's elements so they are seen as Huck would have seen them, a process of imaginative shaping sometimes ignored in that flood of comment which seems to assume that Twain is merely recapturing his own experiences, that Huck Finn is Sam Clemens. Twain's mastery of point of view can be seen in his two accounts of the problem of traffic on the river. In *Life on the Mississippi*, we get a pilot's-eye view. From the majestic altitude of the steamboat pilothouse, the humble rafts, barges, and trading scows which clogged the Mississippi were a continual menace. Pilots had to be constantly alert for the tramp craft which ran at night without required lights. When a steamboat came dangerously close, through no fault of its own, such tramps were likely to throw a "tempest of missiles," even bullets, and treat the steamboat to a dosage of backwoods profanity: "Whar'n the——you goin' to! Cain't you see nothin', you dash-dashed aig-suckin', sheep-stealin', one-eyed son of a stuffed monkey!"[13]

[13] *Life on the Mississippi, The Writings of Mark Twain* (New York: Harper & Bros., 1929), XII, 87–88; orig. pub. 1883. The chapters of *Life on the Mississippi* dealing with Twain's apprenticeship on the river (chs. 4–17, including the passage quoted above) were first published as "Old Times on the Mississippi" in the *Atlantic Monthly*, January–June, August, 1875.

In *Huckleberry Finn* ex-pilot Twain uses the same material—an accidental river meeting between raft and steamboat—but dramatically reverses the viewpoint to make the steamboat the villain (in Huck's eyes):

We could hear her pounding along, but we didn't see her good till she was close. She aimed right for us. Often they do that and try to see how close they can come without touching; sometimes the wheel bites off a sweep, and then the pilot sticks his head out and laughs, and thinks he's mighty smart. . . . All of a sudden she bulged out, big and scary, with a long row of wide-open furnace doors shining like red-hot teeth, and her monstrous bows and guards hanging right over us. There was a yell at us, and a jingling of bells to stop the engines, a pow-wow of cussing, and whistling of steam—and as Jim went overboard on one side and I on the other, she come smashing straight through the raft.[14]

The unique success of *Adventures of Huckleberry Finn* is not simply a result of presenting all of the materials of the novel from Huck's angle of vision or of Twain's use of vernacular. First-person novels have been standard ever since the eighteenth-century exploits of Moll Flanders and Pamela Andrews. Literary interest in American vernacular originated in the 1830's and accelerated in the 1860's—perhaps as a result of the enlarged cultural and geographical perspective which was a by-product of the Civil War. By 1885 readers in America had generously sampled the colloquialisms of Yankees, Wolverines, Suckers, mountaineers, Hoosiers, Creoles, Negroes, Buckeyes, Crackers, and that indigenous American breed of men, half horse and half alligator, who pursued occupations of opportunity along the banks of the Mississippi.

Many readers of *Huckleberry Finn* have felt that its excellence derives from what might be called its harmonies—Huck's integration with the rhythms of nature, the close relation between his observations and his language, the ap-

[14] *Adventures of Huckleberry Finn* (New York: Charles L. Webster & Co., 1885), p. 130. It should be noted that Huck and Jim, responsible raftsmen both, had previously lighted their signal lantern.

propriateness of his moral vision. There is, however, another level of harmony—a stylistic level—since many of Twain's lifelong narrative devices were more appropriate to *Huckleberry Finn* than to any of his other major works. Sam Clemens' four years as a Mississippi steamboat pilot added greatly to the river lore acquired in his Hannibal boyhood and gave the writer who became Mark Twain a store of terminology and imagery which seemed inexhaustible.[15] In some of Twain's nonriver works the employment of such knowledge became decorative or flamboyant (Jim Smiley's dog, for example, is described as having a lower jaw like the forecastle of a steamboat and teeth like furnaces), but its use was entirely relevant in a story which drew much of its inspiration from the river. Huck is an expert on the "June rise" and its drifting treasures, on sandbars and towheads, and the delicate art of navigating the ever-shifting Mississippi currents; much of the novel is based on such river lore. These details will support the most minute examination (unlike those of Cooper's work, which Twain condemned "because the inaccuracy of the details throws a sort of air of fictitiousness and general improbability over it").[16] Huck and Jim escape from Jackson's Island on the raft at one o'clock in the morning and run until dawn, about four hours (ch. 12). They land on a towhead "sixteen or seventeen mile below the village." These figures are precisely substantiated when Huck notes, later on, that the current is something over four miles an hour. They continue to drift seven or eight hours each night, and at this rate it would take five nights to travel the one hundred fifty miles to St. Louis. The reader who keeps an eye on navigation is rewarded to find that on "the fifth night we passed St. Louis."

[15] In *Life on the Mississippi*, Twain remarked that "I loved the profession [piloting] far better than any I have followed since, and I took a measureless pride in it" (p. 118). Twain is perhaps half joking, but half joking is, after all, also half serious.

[16] "Fenimore Cooper's Literary Offenses," *North American Review*, CLXI (July 1895), 7.

The details of the Mississippi are closely related to the language of the novel, and river terminology is richly converted into an important element of Huck's vocabulary through his metaphorical imagination. After Pap celebrates his brief reform with a jug of forty-rod in the Judge's spare room, "they had to take soundings before they could navigate it." On dark nights the moon is "off watch," and Jackson's Island rises out of the river "big and dark and solid, like a steamboat without any lights." Huck's dilemma concerning Jim is a "close place." When he has told Mary Jane Wilks the truth about the King and the Duke, he is "over the shoal water." The explanations required by Aunt Sally are "breakers." Mobbing the Wilkses' graveyard, the townspeople "washed over it like an overflow." And the King, confronted with evidence of his duplicity, almost "squshed down like a bluff bank that the river has cut under."

Huck's conversion of river knowledge into vernacular imagery demonstrates the remarkable relationship between character, setting, and language in *Huckleberry Finn*, a relationship far less convincing in Twain's other works. We are only mildly amused when the author-narrator of *The Innocents Abroad*, after a discussion of the refined appointments and distinguished passenger list of the *Quaker City*, tells us incongruously that his stateroom did not have room "to swing a cat in."[17] When the author-narrator of the *Autobiography*, in a section on business and publishing, explains that Charlie Webster did not need an editorial suite but only an office "with room to swing a cat in,"[18] we simply take note of another slam at the pretensions of Twain's nephew-in-law. But when Huck describes "a log cabin in the edge of the woods, away on the bank on t'other side of the river, being a wood-yard, likely, and piled by them cheats so you can throw a dog through it anywheres" (p. 158), the reader experiences a remarkable harmony of point of view and content.

---

[17] *Writings*, I, 13.
[18] *Autobiography*, ed. Neider, p. 269.

Mark Twain's interest in the vernacular can be seen in his career as a lecturer; the *Autobiography* is filled with practical tips on the precise verbal nuances to entertain, surprise, and outrage an audience for its own delight. His lecturing reveals another lifelong technique, another link between platform and book, which is especially appropriate to *Huckleberry Finn*—the pose of innocence. Many of Twain's best stage tricks involved the mask of naïveté. In "How to Tell a Story" he discusses the use of the "studied remark apparently without knowing it" and the value of being "innocently unaware."[19] The deadpan manner was a pose which Twain used throughout his career: in his writing, on the stage, and in his Hartford living room. The author-narrators of many early works—*The Innocents Abroad*, *Roughing It*, "Old Times on the Mississippi"—are naïve, although not consistently so.[20] Even the jaded, cigar-smoking, world-weary author-narrator of the *Autobiography* drops studied remarks, presumably without being aware of their implications. At their best, these understated remarks are attached, with proper pauses, to the end of a paragraph, where they explode like a string of delayed firecrackers. Twain tells how, as a boy, he used to abuse his mother's trust by concealing a bat in his pocket:

When I said, "There's something in my coat pocket for you," she would put her hand in. But she always took it out again, herself; I didn't have to tell her. It was remarkable the way she couldn't

[19] "How to Tell a Story," *Writings*, XXIV, 267.

[20] The autobiographical poses of these narrators are also not strictly autobiographical. Mark Twain tells us on the first page of *Roughing It* that "I was young and ignorant, and . . . I never had been away from home." He would have us believe that Brigham Young placed his hand upon young Sam's head and said to Orion: "Ah—your child, I presume? Boy or girl?" (*Writings*, III, 97). Sam was twenty-six at the time, and a veteran steamboat pilot. Twain's autobiographical narrators (and characters, as in "The Private History of a Campaign That Failed") are almost always younger than Sam Clemens was during the events they record, a tendency which shows Twain's predilection for the naïve manner.

learn to like private bats. The more experience she had the more she could not change her views.[21]

This control of understatement is not consistently maintained in the *Autobiography* or in many of Twain's other writings, but in *Adventures of Huckleberry Finn*, the pose of innocence is perfectly expressed through the point of view of an unsophisticated fourteen-year-old boy. Huck is Twain's only narrator for whom the naïve pose is totally and consistently appropriate.[22]

As a naïve narrator, Huck gives his author another advantage. He is an effective medium for the expression of the satirical, anticonventional barbs Mark Twain delighted in. Like his humor, Twain's satire can be uncomfortably obvious. But Huck's ignorance prevents him from making evaluations of the villainy and stupidity he reports. The judgments—as well as the elbow nudges and guffaws—are

[21] *Autobiography*, ed. Neider, p. 9.

[22] There are some variations in Huck's naïveté. The boy who is deceived by the King and the Duke (the King "cried and took on so, that me and Jim didn't know hardly what to do, we was so sorry— and so glad and proud we'd got him with us, too"—p. 165) seems to age quickly in the space of a single page ("It didn't take me long to make up my mind that these liars warn't no kings nor dukes, at all, but just low-down humbugs and frauds"—p. 166). Huck's credulity at the circus and with Tom Sawyer ("I didn't believe we could lick such a crowd of Spaniards and A-rabs, but I wanted to see the camels and elephants") is not precisely consistent with his quick wit and perception at other times. But these variations are minor and do not approach the unfortunate inconsistency in point of view which appears in some of Twain's works. In "The Private History of a Campaign That Failed," also published in 1885, the reader is amused by the author-narrator's genial discussion of a good-natured, romantic soldier named Dunlap, who ennobled his plebeian name by spelling it d'Un Lap. Then the tone is inexplicably shattered by the author-narrator's remark about "the ass with the French name." John Gerber seems entirely correct when he notes that Huck is in a sense stronger than Twain; that he provides a "point of view that offers both the curbs and the detachment" that Twain needed for his best efforts ("The Relation between Point of View and Style in the Works of Mark Twain," p. 158).

made by the reader, instead of at him. Thus *Huckleberry Finn* exemplifies the realists' movement away from editorializing, and it fulfills Twain's own definition of the humorous story (a "high and delicate art") which he opposes to the merely comic story (ruined by the teller who invariably slams home the point: "He italicizes it, puts some whooping exclamation-points after it, and sometimes explains it in a parenthesis").[23]

The satire of *Huckleberry Finn* extends over a remarkably wide range. At its highest level Twain attacks the social attitudes in the prewar Mississippi Valley which denied common humanity to the Negro. It is not essentially a question of hostility to the Negro, although that attitude is ridiculed in Pap's political oration ("I was just about to go and vote, myself, if I warn't too drunk to get there; but when they told me there was a State in this country where they'd let that nigger vote, I drawed out"—p. 50). Twain's main concern is to show that inhumanity is a subtle evil, that the degradation of the Negro in the Mississippi Valley was more a product of the indifference of the Aunt Sallys than the brutality of the Simon Legrees:

> "We blowed out a cylinder-head."
> "Good gracious! anybody hurt?"
> "No'm. Killed a nigger."
> "Well, it's lucky; because sometimes people do get hurt."[24]

Huck is glad to see Jim on Jackson's Island ("I warn't lonesome, now"), and he immediately identifies with him

[23] "How to Tell a Story," pp. 264–265. The comic story, said Twain, "is very depressing, and makes one want to renounce joking and lead a better life" (p. 265).

[24] *Huckleberry Finn*, p. 280. The pervasive force of convention is described in Twain's *Autobiography*: "In my schoolboy days I had no aversion to slavery. I was not aware that there was anything wrong about it. No one arraigned it in my hearing; the local papers said nothing against it; the local pulpit taught us that God approved it, that it was a holy thing and that the doubter need only look in the Bible if he wished to settle his mind" (p. 7).

("They're after us!"), but he continues to repeat half-heartedly the clichés of a deformed conscience. Twain's satire thus reaches through Huck to probe the social structure of the Mississippi Valley:

Here was this nigger which I had as good as helped to run away, coming right out flat-footed and saying he would steal his children—children that belonged to a man I didn't even know; a man that hadn't ever done me no harm. [p. 124]

I do believe he cared just as much for his people as white folks does for their'n. It don't seem natural, but I reckon it's so. [p. 201]

Twain's thematic statement of brotherhood is twofold. It is made obliquely, through the satirical destruction of conventional attitudes, and directly, through Huck's fellowship with Jim. Huck never learns to generalize about humanity, slavery, or the Negro, but he does learn that Jim is a human being, that he is "white inside."

Mississippi Valley religion provided an important prop for slavery and another target for Twain's satire. Huck distinguishes several varieties: there is the religion of the Widow Douglas with its mouth-watering Providence, the grim asceticism of Miss Watson, the orgiastic hallelujahs of the Pokeville camp meeting, and the farm preaching of Silas Phelps, who "never charged nothing for his preaching, and it was worth it, too." None of these varieties appeals to Huck. He does not reject religion totally, but he is unwilling to practice a piety which condemns Jim to slavery, one which can't even produce fishhooks through prayer: "Once I got a fish-line, but no hooks. It warn't any good to me without hooks. I tried for the hooks three or four times, but somehow I could't make it work" (p. 29). Huck is unable to theorize about the inadequacies of nineteenth-century religious beliefs, but his sound heart makes such theorizing unnecessary: he will go to hell for his friend.

Slavery and religion are simply the beginning. Twain focuses Huck's innocent eye (and the reader's mature understanding) on romanticism, superstition, sentimentality; and especially on the ignorance, greed, and cruelty of the people who live in Pokeville, Brickesville, Pikesville, and the other "shackly" towns along the Mississippi.[25] *Adventures of Huckleberry Finn* is a satirical anthology. Twain ridicules fortunetelling (Jim's hair ball); father-to-son advice ("If I catch you about that school I'll tan you good. First you know you'll get religion, too. I never see such a son"); nineteenth-century parlors (clay parrots, crockery dogs and cats, turkey-wing fans, and artificial fruit); feuding ("and by-and-by everybody's killed off, and there ain't no more feud"); river-town loafers (whittling and chawing "and gaping and yawning and stretching—a mighty ornery lot"); poetry of the lugubrious American graveyard school ("Ode to Stephen Dowling Bots, Dec'd."); and undertakers ("He was the softest, glidingest stealthiest man I ever see; and there warn't no more smile to him than there is to a ham"). The list is virtually endless, and the satire is endlessly effective.

Irony, like satire, is a product of point of view. *Adventures of Huckleberry Finn* is a continuously ironic book, since the reader's awareness is continuously different from Huck's. The use of the naïve narrator provides the disproportion and incongruity on which irony depends. The ironic vision, necessarily, is split vision. Twain's irony in the novel works on many levels, although not, for the most part, on the primary level of verbal irony. *Huckleberry Finn* is relatively free of the puns and verbal twists of Mark Twain's other works, largely because such word play implies perception and sophistication on the part of the user. The punster is in on the joke, as are the author-narrators of *Roughing It*, *The Innocents Abroad*, and the *Autobiography*. In order to preserve his naïveté and the integrity of his role as a character-narrator, Huck must be outside the joke.

25 Twain's names capture the one-horse quality of such actual river towns as Brownsville, Woodville, Perryville, and Centreville. Brickeys (Arkansas) and Wilkinson (Mississippi) may have suggested Brickesville and the Wilks brothers. Pikesville is perhaps an etymological descendant of mythical Pike County.

Although it neglects verbal irony, *Adventures of Huckleberry Finn*, like most realistic novels, is rich in situational irony. Huck and Jim's freedom ride carries them ever deeper into slave country. Tom's elaborate escape at the novel's end is contrived for a prisoner who had previously been freed. And black Jim, we come to realize, is the whitest man on the river. Within these large structural ironies are smaller, complementary ironic situations. Jim's pious owner, Miss Watson, resolves to sell him down the river. The love between Sophia Grangerford and Harney Shepherdson results in the brutal fish-in-the-barrel shooting of two wounded boys as they attempt to swim to safety. Tom Sawyer experiences his happiest moment when he is shot in the leg—a literal rendering of romantic agony.

As these ironies unfold and deepen, it becomes clear there is yet another level in *Adventures of Huckleberry Finn*. Twain is not merely a user of the techniques of irony; he is an ironist. Like Sophocles, Shakespeare, and Swift, he believes that ultimately man is an ironic creature, a strange combination of power and impotence, nobility and evil, beauty and disease. Twain translates Hamlet's soliloquy on man (noble in reason, infinite in faculties, and the quintessence of dust) into Jim's Missouri Negro dialect: "Dey's two angels hoverin' roun' 'bout him. One uv 'em is white en shiny, en 'tother one is black. De white one gits him to go right, a little while, den de black one sail in en bust it all up. A body can't tell, yit, which one gwyne to fetch him at de las'."[26]

It was Mark Twain's growing awareness of the incongruity between the white angel and the black, between man's potentialities and his performance, which was largely responsible for his increasingly bleak outlook. The seeds of

[26] *Huckleberry Finn*, p. 37. Jim's white and black angelology, itself ironic, shows Twain's awareness of one of the recurrent problems in American race relations—Negro adoption of white attitudes, symbols, and clichés concerning the Negro. Twain investigated the problem in depth in *Pudd'nhead Wilson* (1894).

Twain's late pessimism can be found in *Huckleberry Finn*; the ripened bitter fruit is contained in "The Man That Corrupted Hadleyburg" (1899), "To the Person Sitting in Darkness" (1901), *What Is Man?* (1906), and such posthumous publications as "The Mysterious Stranger" and *Letters from the Earth.* In one of his letters Satan explicitly defines the irony of the human condition: "Man is a marvelous curiosity. When he is at his very very best he is a sort of low grade nickel-plated angel; at his worst he is unspeakable, unimaginable; and first and last and all the time he is a sarcasm. Yet he blandly and in all sincerity calls himself the 'noblest work of God.' "[27]

Much of the voluminous commentary concerning Mark Twain's deepening pessimism is curiously myopic. It turns easily from literary text to biographical speculation and becomes a search for the source and the symbols of Twain's despair. Was it the failure of his publishing firm, the catastrophe of the Paige typesetting machine, daughter Jean's epilepsy, daughter Susy's meningitis, Twain's own bronchitis and rheumatism, his wife's invalidism, old age itself?

---

[27] *Letters from the Earth*, ed. Bernard De Voto (New York: Harper & Row, 1962), p. 7. See De Voto's essay "The Symbols of Despair," given as the William Vaughn Moody Lecture at the University of Chicago in 1940 and included in *Mark Twain at Work* (Cambridge, Mass.: Harvard University Press, 1942).

Howells' deepening thought also turned to the ironies of the human condition, especially those concerned with "the diabolical contrasts of riches and poverty" (*Life in Letters of William Dean Howells*, ed. Mildred Howells [Garden City, N.Y.: Doubleday, Doran & Co., 1928], II, 154). In 1888 Howells wrote to James that America "seems to be the most grotesquely illogical thing under the sun. . . . After fifty years of optimistic content with 'civilization' and its ability to come out all right in the end, I now abhor it, and feel that it is coming out all wrong in the end, unless it bases itself anew on a real equality. Meantime, I wear a fur-lined overcoat, and live in all the luxury my money can buy" (*ibid.*, I, 417). In *Silas Lapham* Bromfield Corey and Miss Kingsbury contrast the great, cool, empty houses of the vacationing rich and the stifling "holes and dens" of Boston's poor, a contrast that Howells first noted in a letter to his father (*ibid.*, I, 363–364).

These personal disasters are relevant, but they are not con-clusive. What was wrong with Mark Twain, the critic asks, ignoring the question that Twain really poses in *Huckleberry Finn* and later works: What is wrong with mankind? This, perhaps, is the ultimate irony of Twain's career. It is one he undoubtedly would have appreciated—thoroughly char-acteristic of the damned human race.

Mark Twain's attacks on convention and stupidity con-tinued and deepened after *Adventures of Huckleberry Finn*, but they were rarely so effective, largely because he never again achieved the same control over point of view. All of the elements discussed above—river lore, the vernacular, the naïve pose, satire, irony—are fundamental to Twain's life-long narrative technique, even to his personality. But only in *Huckleberry Finn*, with its river setting and its first-person narration by a naïve boy, free from the distorting filters of convention, is each element completely relevant to the story. Only in this novel do all of the elements blend together to produce the stylistic harmony of a masterpiece.

While Mark Twain was engaged in shaping the Mississippi Valley through Huck's eyes, Henry James was also exper-imenting with first-person narration. In "The Point of View" (privately printed in 1882), James attempted a miniaturized *Ring and the Book* on what he called the "Americano-European legend." All eight sections consist of letters which, like early glass, reflect more of the observer than the scene observed. James followed this tale with "The Impressions of a Cousin" (*Century Magazine*, 1883), in which he re-corded the impressions of Catherine Condit, a cousin who tries to be a disinterested analyst but ultimately interferes in her relative's love affair and ignites one for herself. The tale is presented in the form of Catherine's diary and, like "The Point of View," reveals some awkward management. James has difficulty with the timing and length of diary entries, and the implausible recapitulation of long passages of dialogue. More serious is the disparity between Cath-

THE CENTURY MAGAZINE

CONTENTS FOR FEBRUARY, 1885.

WILLIAM DEAN HOWELLS, 1886

erine's concise, sharply edged conversation and the expansive diary reflections the narrative forces her to make. Her discomfort, and her creator's, are revealed in asides: "It seems strange to me to write it here"; "I scarcely know why I should have written all this."[28]

James continued to experiment periodically with first-person point of view, but he ultimately rejected the form as "foredoomed to looseness" and unfavorable to the "precious discriminations" on which his art is based.[29] First-person narration forced Mark Twain to be more subtle. For James it was not subtle enough—an interesting indication of the difference between the two men. James abandoned first-person technique but not what might be called first-person sensibility. The events of his novels and tales are presented as seen by the characters, not as seen from an authorial Olympia. James keeps third-person rhetoric and some of the trappings of the third-person omniscient author; but he does not allow himself the wide-ranging liberties of the omniscient attitude, a discrimination missed by such critics as John Tilford.[30] James tends to intrude verbally but not structurally. He will use conventional phrases, reminiscent of Trollope and Thackeray, such as "the discerning reader," and "my muse." Quoted out of context, these phrases would seem to deny James' antiomniscience. But the full context shows the realistic attitude at work: "I won't take [it] upon myself to say—especially as the discerning reader will be able to judge for himself"; "Whether [Jackson Lemon lives] in hope or fear, to-day, is more than my muse has revealed."[31]

28 *The Complete Tales of Henry James*, ed. Leon Edel (Philadelphia: J. B. Lippincott Co., 1962–64), V, 166, 179.
29 Preface to *The Ambassadors*, in *The Art of the Novel*, pp. 320–321.
30 See "James the Old Intruder," *Modern Fiction Studies*, IV (Summer 1958), 157–164.
31 These examples are drawn from two of James' tales published in 1884, "The Author of *Beltraffio*" and "Lady Barberina" (*Complete Tales*, V, 304, 301).

The opening chapters of *The Bostonians* provide a useful illustration of the Jamesian method. James begins with a conversation between Basil Ransom and Mrs. Luna, Olive Chancellor's sister, while they wait for Olive to appear. James immediately tells us that Basil is "the most important personage in my narrative" and describes him with care. Once Basil has been established, the novel can begin in earnest. The reader now has a point of view, a central consciousness, a reflecting mirror, to give shape to the characters and the action. Olive appears, and we see her as Basil sees her ("The young man was therefore free to look at her"). Olive's parlor, like its owner, is described in the third-person language of the author-narrator, but such third-person exposition is given the stamp of Basil's personality: "The young man, left alone, looked about the parlor." The description is enlarged when Basil takes "a position from which he had another view." Olive and Basil soon leave for Miss Birdseye's, and again the author-narrator prefaces his description of the meeting with the establishment of the point of view: "The first thing Ransom noticed . . . ." A later meeting of the Wednesday Club is reported by Basil, "through whose ears we are listening." Most of the nonscenic portions of the book are conveyed through Basil Ransom's eyes and ears. The Boston reformers are consistently seen from his conservative, unsympathetic, emphatically non-Bostonian point of view. A dichotomy is established between Basil and the Bostonians which structures the narrative development and provides the double vision which makes humor and satire possible.

In *The Bostonians*, as in most of James' works, the presentation of the materials of the novel from the point of view of the characters is not fetishly maintained. It is a question of 90 rather than of 100 per cent. James will occasionally relate things which the characters cannot know and at times speak directly (if somewhat guiltily) to the reader, "to whom in the course of our history I shall be under the neces-

sity of imparting much occult information."[32] Some omniscience, especially in the beginning of a book, is usually
necessary; and, like most realists, James finds omniscience
useful on occasion to make narrative short cuts.

In spite of this qualification James' central artistic purpose
is to present the events of his novels as they are seen by
characters; "not as my own impersonal account of the affair in hand, but as my account of somebody's impression of
it."[33] It is the response of the character to the affair at hand
which interests him most, not the affair. In order to keep the
emphasis on the character's point of view, James weaves
dialogue indirectly into pictorial description. Many passages of third-person exposition are personalized through
the employment of a character's tone of speech or thought.
James' writings are filled with these submerged scenes. At
the beginning of Miss Birdseye's meeting, the author-
narrator reports that "Miss Birdseye expressed the hope
that Miss Chancellor had had [her dinner]; she would have
had plenty of time to take it, for no one had come in yet;
she didn't know what made them all so late" (p. 540). The
passage enables the reader to hear Miss Birdseye saying,
with her usual genial incoherence, "I don't know what has
made them all so late."

In describing Olive's view of the coming revolution, the
author-narrator introduces a new rhetoric:

The unhappiness of women! . . . Ages of oppression had rolled
over them; uncounted millions had lived only to be tortured, to
be crucified. They were her sisters, they were her own, and the
day of their delivery had dawned. This was the only sacred cause;
this was the great, the just revolution. It must triumph, it must

[32] *The Bostonians, Century Magazine,* XXIX (February 1885), 532.
The realists are always concerned about how the narrator or central
consciousness gets his information. When Huck repeats the Duke's
version of Hamlet's soliloquy, he is careful to tell us that "I learned
it, easy enough, while he was learning it to the king" (p. 179).
[33] *Art of the Novel,* p. 327.

sweep everything before it; it must exact from the other, the brutal, blood-stained, ravening race, the last particle of expiation! . . . It would be a new era . . . and the names of those who had helped to show the way and lead the squadrons would be the brightest in the tables of fame. [p. 543]

The point of view here is obviously not Basil's or James', both of whom are suspicious of reformers (to Basil, reformers are "mediums, communists, vegetarians"). It is Olive's point of view of Olive, conveyed in phrases which capture her inflamed revolutionary imagination. It is Olive, triumphantly mounted upon the lecture platform of her own mind.

James' ability to give the imprint of character to the pictures painted in the third person by the author-narrator can also be seen in *The Princess Casamassima*. When Hyacinth Robinson visits the Princess at her country estate, that miracle of green thoughts and brick chimneys is reported through "our hero's cockney vision." When the author-narrator discusses Hyacinth's friend Millicent, he quietly inserts fragments of her speech: "She told Hyacinth it was a 'shime' to bring a young lady to the play when you had n't so much as an opera-glass for her to look at the company."[34] In describing the domicile of M. Poupin, an exiled French revolutionary, the author-narrator subtly increases his use of French words and phrases. Poupin is Hyacinth's *parrain*. They both work for *le vieux* Mr. Crookenden and suffer the *désagrément* of poverty. Madame Poupin, wearing the cap of an *ouvrière*, makes *tisane*. Her cooking is *cuisine*, prepared in the *intérieur*.

The author-narrator of *The Princess Casamassima* notes that Hyacinth knew the vocabulary of his friends by heart and "could have said everything, in the same words" that they were likely to say on any occasion. James' author-narrators also have this ability, and their adoption of the vocabulary of the fictional characters tends to integrate

[34] *Atlantic Monthly*, LVI (December 1885), 723.

"picture" and "scene," to keep the emphasis precisely where James wants it—on the character's point of view.[35]

Howells also rejects the tradition of omniscience in fiction by concentrating on scenic presentation and eliminating the omniscient attitude from third-person exposition. All of his novels in the 1880's depend heavily on scenes and dialogue, a fact that can be verified simply by opening the books at random. Most pages have a fragmented appearance, caused by the frequent paragraph indentations required by dialogue. In *Indian Summer*, there are only eight pages in the entire novel which do not contain dialogue. The first chapter of *The Rise of Silas Lapham* is approximately the same length as the first four introductory chapters of *Waverley*. Howells' chapter contains 122 paragraphs; Scott's four chapters have only 34.

Howells relied so much on the "dramatic method" that even Henry James—a forceful advocate of the method and the inventor of the term—thought he had gone too far. In a *Harper's Weekly* article in June, 1886 (after the appearance of *Silas Lapham* and *Indian Summer*, and during the serialization of *The Minister's Charge*), James inserted a mild rebuke in the midst of perceptive praise, noting ironically that Howells had difficulty with dialogue in the early stages of his career:

He believed, in particular, that he could not make people talk, and such have been the revenges of time that a cynical critic might almost say of him to-day that he cannot make them keep

[35] In *Mark Twain: The Development of a Writer* (Cambridge, Mass.: Harvard University Press, 1962, p. 121) Henry Nash Smith notes that Huck sometimes uses the phraseology of another character. Huck, for example, reports the following version of the King's "tears and flapdoodle" speech to the mourners in the Wilks parlor: "By-and-by the king . . . slobbers out a speech . . . about its being a sore trial for him and his poor brother to lose the diseased, and to miss seeing diseased alive . . . but its a trial that's sweetened and sanctified to us by this dear sympathy and these holy tears" (*Huckleberry Finn*, pp. 212–213).

silent. . . . He has an increasing tendency to tell his story altogether in conversations, so that a critical reader sometimes wishes, not that the dialogue might be suppressed (it is too good for that), but that it might be distributed, interspaced with narrative and pictorial matter. The author forgets sometimes to paint, to evoke the conditions and appearances, to build in the subject. He is doubtless afraid of doing these things in excess, having seen in other hands what disastrous effects that error may have.[36]

Howells' dramatic, conversational method is nowhere seen more clearly than in the opening chapter of *The Rise of Silas Lapham*, which avoids the traditional introductory blocks of omniscient exposition. Half of the chapter is dialogue, and much of the rest is devoted to dialogue support ("Silas said"; "queried Bartley, with his pencil poised above his note-book") and to quotations from Bartley Hubbard's interview in the *Events*. The strategy of the chapter shows the realist at work. The novel begins in Lapham's fifty-fifth year, at the peak of his business career, in order to focus primarily on the brief period which illuminates his entire life. Howells is thus faced with a dual problem. He must sketch in the background for the reader: Silas' obscure beginnings in northern Vermont, the discovery of the mineral paint mine on his father's farm, and his early business career, including the partner Silas uses and then discards. In addition, Howells must give some indication of Lapham's character—a product of his experience and the key factor in the fall/rise that the novel documents.

All this is accomplished, at a stroke, by having Lapham

---

[36] *Harper's Weekly*, XXX (19 June 1886), 394–395. James' willingness to be the "cynical critic" and the "critical reader," even in regard to the writings of his friend and fellow realist, shows the difference in the criticism of the two men. Howells is a partisan, getting in blows for realism whenever he can and largely concerned with the general aims of realistic fiction. James is more detached, less propagandistic, further from the battlefield. Concentrating on technique, James makes finer discriminations and tends to balance his judgments more carefully.

interviewed for a newspaper feature article. Lapham's present position is indicated immediately—he is being interviewed for the "Solid Men of Boston" series, and reporter Bartley Hubbard tells Silas frankly that he is "just one million times more interesting to the public than if [he] hadn't a dollar." Lapham's past is adroitly brought out in the course of the interview. Howells wants to get Lapham's barefoot background on record, unapologetically (Howells himself had come a long way from Martins Ferry, Ohio), but without getting the author-narrator entangled in the clichés of *Ragged Dick* or *Mark, the Match Boy*. Thus while Silas treats his farm boyhood and his poor-but-honest parents with seriousness and even reverence, the scene is unsentimentalized by Bartley Hubbard's astringent cynicism, an attitude that is appropriate both to Bartley's previous fictional career in *A Modern Instance* and to his occupation as a journalist:

"I was born on a farm, and—"
"Worked in the fields summers and went to school winters: regulation thing?" Bartley cut in.
"Regulation thing," said Lapham, accepting this irreverent version of his history somewhat dryly.
"Parents poor, of course," suggested the journalist. "Any barefoot business? Early deprivations of any kind, that would encourage the youthful reader to go and do likewise?"[37]

Lapham's character is established dramatically in the first chapter. He gives his left hand to Bartley without rising, kicks the door shut with his huge foot, pounds his correspondence with a "great hairy fist," says "cut" for coat and "rud" for road, and brags about covering the landscape with Lapham's mineral paint ("There wa'n't a board-fence, nor a bridge-girder, nor a dead wall, nor a barn, nor a face of rock in that whole region that didn't have 'Lapham's Mineral Paint—Specimen' on it in . . . three colors"—p. 17). It is

[37] *Century Magazine*, XXIX (November 1884), 13.

soon clear that Silas Lapham is an uncouth, aggressive, over-bearing, and ungrammatical New American, whose religion is business and whose philosophy is materialism.

The point of view in the first chapter is Bartley Hubbard's, and his portrait of Silas is largely negative. The few sections of third-person exposition are colored by the journalist's at-titude and by his rhetoric. Adopting Bartley's tone, the author-narrator notes that Lapham's family photograph shows the old farmhouse, "whose original ugliness had been smartened up with a coat of Lapham's own paint and heightened with an incongruous piazza." The chapter ends appropriately with a scene in the Hubbard household.

Chapter 2 rapidly changes point of view, a change neatly indicated by the first sentence: "After dropping Bartley Hubbard at the *Events* building, Lapham drove on." Having served his turn upon the stage, Bartley is dropped—at the *Events* building and out of the novel for good. Commencing with the second chapter the focus is on Silas, and the reader develops a sympathy for him that is not possible in chap-ter 1. Much of the rest of the book is devoted to showing the other side of the negative qualities which are presented, and then taken for granted, at the novel's outset. Silas is un-couth, but he is also honest and candid. He is aggressive and has treated his former partner roughly, but he makes amends by helping him financially (Silas also quietly supports the family of a deceased Civil War comrade). Lapham is un-grammatical, but his language, as well as his character, often seems stronger than that of the exquisitely grammatical flower of Bostonian decadence, Bromfield Corey. And al-though Lapham is overbearing in his success, he bears up well under a series of business and personal disasters.

The reader's sympathetic understanding of Silas (we un-derstand him "down to the ground, inside and out," James said[38]) is the result of the concentrated focus established after the first chapter. Most of the rest of the book consists

---

[38] "William Dean Howells," *Harper's Weekly*, XXX (19 June 1886), 394.

of scenes involving Silas as businessman and father, scenes in which Silas is discussed, summaries of what Silas is thinking, and commentaries on Silas' position made by the author-narrator. In spite of his faults and his lack of heroic stature, Silas—like other protagonists in realistic fiction—enlists our sympathy and our respect partly because we get to know him so well. As Robert Frost observed, it is difficult to hate people up close.[39]

Howells, like James and Mark Twain, relies heavily on the scenic method. He also, on occasion, adopts the tone and phraseology of his characters when using the third-person voice of the author-narrator. The reader can hear Silas speaking through many third-person summaries: "For himself, he owned that he had made mistakes; he could see just where the mistakes were—put his finger right on them. But one thing he could say: he had been no man's enemy but his own; every dollar, every cent had gone to pay his debts; he had come out with clean hands."[40] But Howells does not go so far as James or Twain in controlling point of view and screening commentary and descriptive matter through the consciousnesses of characters. A few passages in each Howells novel seem suspiciously omniscient and intrusive, such as the discussion of marriage which begins the fourth chapter of *The Rise of Silas Lapham* ("The silken texture of the marriage tie bears a daily strain of wrong and insult to which no other human relation can be subjected without lesion"). Nevertheless, such passages are rare and when they occur they tend to be generalizations which arise from the context of the novels rather than abstractions

---

[39] A more exaggerated and apparently unintentional example can be seen in *Babbitt*. Sinclair Lewis is determined to damn his protagonist, but he is only partially successful because of the depth of his portrait. Conversely, characters who are not illuminated by the spotlight of point of view are often negative or mysterious. We rarely share Olive Chancellor's thoughts, and it is easy to make her a villain. The Princess Casamassima is a figure of some mystery because we generally see her only from Hyacinth's point of view.

[40] *Century Magazine*, XXX (August 1885), 524.

superimposed upon them. Like James and Twain, Howells demonstrates variety and flexibility in his handling of point of view. The realists refuse to be bound by iron formulas, and their practice shows differences in emphasis and in degree. Such differences, however, only serve to backlight the essential feature that unites the realists and controls much of their fiction—the rejection of the omniscient point of view.

CHAPTER VI

A MORE COMPLICATED PLACE

Realistic Complexity and Multiplicity

ACCORDING to Van Wyck Brooks, 1915 is the date that marks America's coming-of-age. Brooks is wrong by half a century; the Civil War marked the real end of American innocence and the tentative beginnings of a complex new American fiction. Henry James, Mark Twain, and Howells had difficulty converting the war into imaginative literature, but they were acutely aware of its effects. James, in particular, found the war the dividing line between Hawthorne's age and his own:

One may say that the Civil War marks an era in the history of the American mind. It introduced into the national consciousness a certain sense of proportion and relation, of the world being a more complicated place than it had hitherto seemed, the future more treacherous, success more difficult. . . . [The] American, in days to come, will be a more critical person than his complacent and confident grandfather. He has eaten of the tree of knowledge.[1]

To be sure, many innocent Americans appear in post–Civil War fiction—witness Daisy Miller, Christopher Newman, Lambert Strether, Lemuel Barker, Isabel Archer, Huck Finn, Silas Lapham, and Theodore Colville—but the most interesting aspect of their innocence is that it inevitably becomes enmeshed in the complex web of experience. And that experience is not limited to Europe or to the melodra-

---

[1] Henry James, *Hawthorne* (New York: Harper & Bros., 1879), pp. 139–140.

matic machinations of aristocratic Bellegardes or socialistic Hoffendahls. Blake's tiger is indigenous to the new world too, and his brightly burning eyes are reflected in the violent glare of Colonel Sherburn, the casual inhumanity of Aunt Sally, the pathetic greed of Mr. Rogers, and the murderous battlefield exchanges between Americans which convince Captain Colburne (and Captain De Forest) that the American past is dead—as dead as the six hundred thousand men who fell at Bull Run, Shiloh, Chancellorsville, Chickamauga, Gettysburg, and the other graveyards of American innocence.

Just as the realists' handling of point of view seems to derive from their commitment to antiomniscience, other techniques are related to the realists' concern with the complications of life in America after the Civil War—complications caused by the shock of fratricide, lingering sectional hostilities, rapid industrialization, urbanization, immigration, internal migration, economic dislocation, and intensified by the agnostic and scientific erosion of comfortable habits of traditional thought. Late nineteenth-century America became a more complicated place. The optimistic answers of the previous generation were undercut by strong currents of complexity and multiplicity. A distinction between the terms is useful: complexity refers to the interwoven, entangled density of experience; multiplicity indicates the simultaneous existence of different levels of reality (or many truths, equally "true" from some point of view). These were the intellectual conditions which broke Henry Adams' historical neck and made his education irrelevant. The irony in the title of *The Education of Henry Adams* was explained by the book's subtitle: *A Study of Twentieth-Century Multiplicity.*

Much realistic fiction is concerned with the attempt to unravel the complexities and multiplicities of experience. On the last page of *A Modern Instance*, Clara Atherton explicitly states the realists' view: "Of course, it isn't a ques-

tion of mere right and wrong, of gross black and white—
there are degrees, there are shades."[2] Henry James, a wholesale dealer in degrees and shades, agreed: "No themes are
so human as those that reflect for us, out of the confusion
of life, the close connexion of bliss and bale, of the things
that help with the things that hurt."[3] Realistic fiction is devoted to the theme of unsimple truth, a theme which char-
acterizes the realists but is, of course, not peculiar to them.
Unsimple truth plucks at the heart of Hamlet's mystery. And
unsimple truth is the point of Melville's chapter "The Lee
Shore," his symbol of the treacherous comforts of safe, conventional, one-dimensional, simplistic thinking. Shakespeare and Melville would have agreed with Mark Twain,
who expressed the matter in one epigrammatic stroke in
Roughing It: "All our 'information' had three sides to it."[4]

Three-sided information was a challenge and delight to
the flexible mind of William James, perhaps the most representative intellectual theorist of the age. William summarized the realistic position in *Pragmatism*, rejecting "bad
a priori reasons, . . . fixed principles, closed systems, . . .
pretended absolutes and origins, . . . dogma, artificiality, and
the pretence of finality in truth." He argued for a philosophy
that would embrace the open air, a philosophy built on
pluralism, on a "multiverse," claiming that "no theory is
absolutely a transcript of reality, but . . . any one of them
may from some point of view be useful. . . . Ideas (which
themselves are but parts of our experience) become true just

[2] W. D. Howells, *A Modern Instance, Century Magazine*, XXIV
(October 1882), 919. The novel closes on a characteristic note—the
scenic portrayal of complexity: "Atherton flung the letter upon the
table, and drew a troubled sigh. 'Ah, I don't know! I don't know!' "
[3] Preface to *What Maisie Knew*, in *The Art of the Novel*, ed. R. P.
Blackmur (New York: Charles Scribner's Sons, 1934), p. 143.
[4] *The Writings of Mark Twain* (New York: Harper & Bros., 1929),
III, 120. "The Lee Shore" is chapter 23 of *Moby-Dick*. See Willard
Farnham's perceptive discussion of unsimple truth in his introduction to the Penguin Books edition of *Hamlet* (1957).

in so far as they help us to get into satisfactory relation with other parts of our experience."[5]

Long before *Pragmatism* was published, the realists were using similar concepts in their fiction. Huck Finn is a native American pragmatist. His opinions, firmly grounded on his experience, continually deflate the ballooning romanticism of Tom Sawyer, which is based on such fictional authorities as the *Arabian Nights, The Count of Monte Cristo,* and *Le Vicomte de Bragelonne*:

When I start in to steal a nigger, or a watermelon, or a Sunday-school book, I ain't no ways particular how it's done so it's done. What I want is my nigger; or what I want is my watermelon; or what I want is my Sunday-school book; and if a pick's the handiest thing, that's the thing I'm agoing to dig that nigger or that watermelon or that Sunday-school book out with; and I don't give a dead rat what the authorities thinks about it nuther. [p. 310]

David Sewell, the minister in Howells' *The Minister's Charge; or, The Apprenticeship of Lemuel Barker*, also comes into conflict with the authorities. When his wife accuses him of deserting his fixed moral principles, Sewell answers pragmatically, "I suppose I was trying to adapt myself to circumstances."[6] Much of the novel documents Sewell's apprenticeship in social relativity.

Henry James made an eloquent plea for pragmatism in fiction in "The Art of Fiction" in 1884, stating that "reality has a myriad forms" and that "experience is never limited and it is never complete."[7] The similarities in the brothers' view of a complex, open-ended universe are made explicit in the letters which William and Henry exchanged late in their lives. Henry, after reading *Pragmatism*, was astonished by the "extent to which all my life I have . . . unconsciously pragmatised." He read William's *A Pluralistic Universe* with

[5] William James, *Pragmatism* (New York: Longmans, Green & Co., 1907), pp. 51, 57–58.

[6] *Century Magazine*, XXXIII (December 1886), 189.

[7] *Longman's Magazine*, IV (September 1884), 509.

"thrilled interest, . . . with enchantment, with pride, and almost with comprehension," and added:

It may sustain and inspire you a little to know that I'm *with* you, all along the line—and can conceive of no sense in any philosophy that is not yours! As an artist and a "creator" I can catch on, hold on, to pragmatism and can work in the light of it and apply it; finding, in comparison, everything else (so far as I know the same!) utterly irrelevant and useless—vainly and coldly parallel![8]

Unilluminated by the bright absolutes of omniscience, the realists work in the subdued, flickering lights of pragmatism. Since the pragmatist cannot accept given, universal truths, he must be concerned with what man knows and how he learns. The problems of vision, knowledge, illusion, and the relation of appearance to reality form a significant part of pragmatic considerations. This is as true for fiction as it is for philosophy, and the novels and stories of the mid-1880's are filled with questions of "seeing" and "knowing," and, of course, not "seeing" and not "knowing." In "The Impressions of a Cousin," cousin Catherine expresses her condemnation of Mrs. Ermine in visual terms: "She doesn't see what she looks at. . . . She sees nothing that really occurs, and gazes complacently into the void."[9] Huck Finn would be a little edgy in Catherine's Fifty-third Street parlor, but he looks at the world in remarkably similar terms. Upon reflection, Huck realizes that dogs don't eat watermelon and therefore the scraps carried off from the Phelps' table are destined for a human being, for Jim: "It shows how a body can see and don't see at the same time."[10]

Seeing accurately is the beginning of knowledge, a relationship which is capsulized by the common use of "I see"

[8] F. O. Matthiessen, *The James Family* (New York: Alfred A. Knopf, 1947), pp. 343–344.

[9] *The Complete Tales of Henry James*, ed. Leon Edel (Philadelphia: J. B. Lippincott Co., 1962–64), V, 116, 163.

[10] *Adventures of Huckleberry Finn* (New York: Charles L. Webster & Co., 1885), p. 293.

for "I understand." James, Mark Twain, and Howells generally subscribe to the twentieth-century belief that understanding is an active process, that knowledge is a question of making relations. The tree falling unheard in the forest is, for the realists, an impossible situation—one without a point of view. Thus the American literary realists, somewhat ironically, are not philosophical realists.[11] They do not believe in a reality independent from its presentation to the consciousness. They have, as Harry Levin observes, "kept open the question 'What is truth?' "[12] and much of their fiction probes the complexity of human knowledge. James' tale "The Tree of Knowledge" is an appropriate symbol, and its dialogue echoes through the writings of the mid-1880's:

"He'll *know*."
"Ah, but *what* will he know?"

"I see."
"No, you don't see—yet. But you will—"

"I know now. . . . It *isn't* so very good to know."
"Are you very sure you do know?"
"Well, I at least know about as much as I can bear."

"She *does* know?"
"She has always, always known."

[11] Everett Carter disagrees, claiming that the realists derive from the Scottish philosophy of common sense, that "they never doubted that they need do anything else than observe carefully and honestly and report truthfully in order to arrive at truthfulness, and hence beauty, in fiction" (*Howells and the Age of Realism* [Philadelphia, J. B. Lippincott Co., 1954], p. 89). This is somewhat more true of Howells than of James, but even for Howells, seeing accurately is only the beginning and to see is not necessarily to understand. Professor Carter perhaps underestimates the realistic commitment to relativity and complexity, and the growth of Howells' thought. Indeed, Professor Carter's statement sounds much like early Howells, and it is interesting that Carter supports it with statements made by Howells in 1867 and 1871.

[12] "What Is Realism?" *Contexts of Criticism* (New York: Atheneum, 1963), p. 75.

Yours till death.
Henry James

HENRY JAMES, 1882

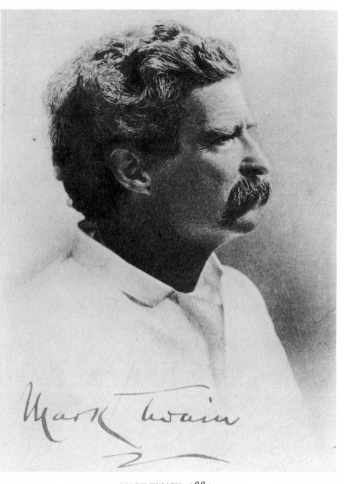

MARK TWAIN, 1884

Between puffs on his pipe, Peter Brench utters the benediction for this and many another realistic tale: "It isn't knowledge, it's ignorance that—as we've been beautifully told—is bliss."[13]

The realists' concern with the complexity and multiplicity of knowledge and experience is expressed by their extensive use of ambiguity. "The *whole* of anything is never told," James wrote in his notebook, "you can only take what groups together."[14] The realistic novels make no attempt to tell the whole of anything; many aspects are deliberately left in the ambiguous half-lights of what groups together. The question of reform—central to both *The Bostonians* and *The Princess Casamassima*—is unresolved. The reader cannot side with the apocalyptic feminism of Olive Chancellor, but neither can he accept Basil Ransom's reactionary doctrines (they are, as a magazine editor noted in his rejection of an article submitted by Basil, "about three hundred years behind the age; doubtless some magazine of the sixteenth century would have been very happy to print them").[15]

It is impossible to judge either the strength or the validity of the revolutionary movement in *The Princess Casamassima*. The anarchic underworld is hinted at rather than depicted, as if the observer had only a hurried glimpse at a shadowy gathering through dim, back-room windows. This impression is substantiated by James' Preface: "The value I wished most to render and the effect I wished most to pro-

[13] *Complete Tales*, XI, 97, 98, 103, 109–110.

[14] *The Notebooks of Henry James*, ed. F. O. Matthiessen and Kenneth B. Murdock (New York: Oxford University Press, 1947), p. 18. Taking the point a step further, James notes in the Preface to *The Princess Casamassima* that complexity and ambiguity make serious fiction possible: "It seems probable that if we were never bewildered there would never be a story to tell about us" (*Art of the Novel*, p. 63).

[15] *Century Magazine*, XXX (July 1885), 434.

duce were precisely those of our not knowing, of society's not knowing, but only guessing and suspecting."[16]

Similarly, the reader has only guesses and suspicions to help him determine the status of the new American in *The Rise of Silas Lapham* and *The Minister's Charge*, and the status of the old Bostonian is equally unclear. Howells seems to side with Bromfield Corey and his brother-in-law Charles Bellingham in their gentlemanly superiority to Silas' drunken garrulity at the Corey dinner party, yet at other times their superiority is depicted as a hollow echo of an out-of-date social code. In *The Minister's Charge* Howells' satire sharpens as Corey and Charles Bellingham visit Lemuel after a street-car accident. Howells paints a vivid picture of Lemuel's fear of amputation, his close contact with the suffering of "broken and mangled men, drunk with ether," and his awareness of the deaths concealed behind white linen screens. Bromfield Corey and his brother-in-law enter the hospital as they would a museum, and their patrician curiosity is singularly out of place:

Corey said [afterward] that the effect of the hospital, with its wards branching from the classistic building in the center, was delightfully Italian; it was like St. Peter's on a small scale, and he had no idea how interesting the South End was; it was quite a bit of foreign travel to go up there. Bellingham had explored the hospital throughout; he said he had found it the thing to do—it was a thing for everybody to do; he was astonished that he had never done it before.[17]

These ambiguous backgrounds and issues are more than matched by the ambiguous endings of realistic works, a characteristic which Howells traced directly to the complexity of knowledge: "I am very often puzzled to know what is the truth, and that may account for the 'stopping-short' which you notice. It is, however, also a matter of artistic

16 *Art of the Novel*, pp. 77–78.
17 *Century Magazine*, XXXIII (December 1886), 188.

preference."[18] The realistic preference, as seen in the endings of the novels of the mid-1880's, revels in the ambiguous and the unresolved. *Huckleberry Finn* seems to stop, rather than conclude. Pap is dead, Jim is free, and the Duke and the King are deservedly, if cruelly, tarred and feathered. But Huck Finn's adventures, true to the picaresque tradition, have changed nothing. Pap is not missed, Jim is freed by an improbable deathbed gesture—not by any new awareness—and the impartial Mississippi will continue to wash down an endless tide of scheming adventurers. Huck ends as he began, lighting out. He is not much different for his experience, and the world he rubs elbows with is unaltered. Huck has come to the realization that Jim is "white inside," but the same Huck answers Aunt Sally's question—"Anybody hurt?"—with "No'm. Killed a nigger." Thus the Tom Sawyerism in the novel's late chapters is justified, if overdone, and Tom's final shenanigans balance those in the early chapters.[19] Nothing has changed, at least for the novel's characters (hopefully the reader has been instructed). *Adventures of Huckleberry Finn* is a depressing humorous book, for the ignorance and dishonesty which it so brilliantly depicts remain unenlightened and unreformed.

[18] From Howells' letter to Thomas Wentworth Higginson on 17 September 1879; quoted by Edwin H. Cady, *The Road to Realism: The Early Years, 1837–1885, of William Dean Howells* (Syracuse: Syracuse University Press, 1956), p. 189. In his notebook entry for *The Portrait of a Lady* James anticipated criticism of the realistic penchant for stopping short: "The obvious criticism of course will be that it is not finished—that I have not seen the heroine to the end of her situation—that I have left her *en l'air.*—This is both true and false" (*Notebooks*, p. 18).

[19] There is a morass of conflicting commentary on this point. See, for example, Leo Marx, "Mr. Eliot, Mr. Trilling, and *Huckleberry Finn*," *American Scholar*, XXII (Autumn 1953), 423–440; Richard P. Adams, "The Unity and Coherence of *Huckleberry Finn*," *Tulane Studies in English*, VI (1956), 87–103; Thomas A. Gullason, "The 'Fatal' Ending of *Huckleberry Finn*," *American Literature*, XXIX (March 1957), 86–91.

The Minister's Charge also ends with what groups together, rather than the whole. It is not clear where Lemuel's
apprenticeship will lead him, and his relationship with
Statira is unresolved. Mrs. Sewell, weary of her husband's
charge, asks, in the closing pages: "And do you think you
have got through with him now?" (p. 191). Sewell's answer
—"I have just begun with him"—summarizes the position
of the realistic author as he takes leave of his characters.
Howells makes the point clear in the last sentence: "[The
reader] may be assured here that the marriage which even-
tually took place was not that of Lemuel and Statira; though
how the union . . . came about, it is aside from the purpose
of this story to tell, and must be left for some future in-
quiry" (p. 192).

Although the ambiguous ending of *The Minister's Charge*
formally meets the realistic specifications, it must be admitted that it is not entirely satisfactory. Howells has Bellingham ridicule romantic conclusions: "In any well-regulated
romance that cough of hers would run into quick consump-
tion and carry Barker's fiancée off in six weeks; and then he
could resume his career of usefulness and . . . marry someone
else" (p. 188). Howells, however, is subtly guilty himself, for
Statira's cough apparently will carry her off, rather implau-
sibly, to a box factory in Philadelphia, and Barker will be
free to resume his career and marry a partner more appropriate to his future than his past. The leading candidate, when
the novel reaches its stopping point, is Miss Jessie Carver, an
attractive art student. Howells thus comes dangerously close
to the happy ending which his realistic theory officially
denounces.[20] But Howells' reasoning in this case can be seen

[20] James, in a discussion of *The Story of a Play*, notes perceptively that there is an occasional gap between Howells' tough-minded
theory and his more graceful and genial practice: "Life, in his pages,
is never too hard, too ugly, passions and perversities never too sharp,
not to allow, on the part of his people, of such an exercise of friendly
wit about each other as may well, when one considers it, minimize
shocks and strains. So it muffles and softens, all around, the edges
of *The Story of a Play*. The mutual indulgences of the whole thing

100

by considering the alternatives. If Lemuel had been unable to escape from Statira—with her vulgar accents, low tastes, and impossible friends—the novel would have become a bloodless *American Tragedy*. Statira, in Howells' inevitable metaphor, is a millstone. But the tragic impulse is as false to Howells' realism as the romantic-sentimental impulse, and the conclusion of *The Minister's Charge* shows the author attempting, characteristically, to steer a middle course. His point of reference is stated once again in the closing paragraph. Lemuel's career, with its complex uncertainties, neither happy nor tragic, has been "offered to the reader as founded in probability and human nature" (p. 192).

Probability and human nature leave problems unsolved in *The Rise of Silas Lapham*. The alliance between Penelope Lapham and Tom Corey could unite the families, but Howells refuses the convenience of such an arrangement and even discusses it explicitly: "It would be easy to point out traits in Penelope's character which finally reconciled all her husband's family and endeared her to them. These things continually happen in novels."[21] But not, Howells might have added, in realistic novels. There is a brief season of civility on the part of the two families, and Lily Corey makes a "little, ineffectual sketch" of Penelope. But "the differences

---

fairly bathe the prospect in something like a suffusion of that 'romantic' to which the author's theory of the novel offers so little hospitality. And that, for the moment, is an odd consummation" (*Literature* [9 July 1898], p. 18; quoted in *Henry James: The American Essays*, ed. Leon Edel [New York: Vintage Books, 1956], pp. 256–257). This tension in Howells' writing can be seen in two remarks in the "Editor's Study": "It is well to call things by their names, even if they are spades" (*Harper's Monthly*, LXXII [January 1886], 322); "Generally, people now call a spade an agricultural implement" (LXXIX [June 1889], 153).

[21] *Century Magazine*, XXX (August 1885), 523. It has to be confessed that this statement, like the final paragraph of *The Minister's Charge*, is spoken by an omniscient author. But Howells, in both passages, is using the weapons of the enemy to good advantage. He employs an omniscient point of view to attack the spirit of omniscient sentimentality which required neat last-chapter resolutions.

remained uneffaced" and both sides are relieved that Tom and Penelope's residence in Mexico will decrease the communication between the families. "At that distance we can —correspond," notes Nanny Corey. Penelope's sharp tongue leaves a final gash as she drives away from her parents-in-law: "I don't think I shall feel strange amongst the Mexicans now" (p. 524).

Henry James, who continually honed the blunt bulk of ambiguity to a razor's edge, appears to resolve both of his novels of the mid-1880's with un-Jamesian resolution. He does not conclude with a characteristic "Well, there you are," as in *The Ambassadors* (leaving the reader wondering just where the devil he and Lambert Strether, in fact, are). *The Bostonians* ends with the traditional grace note of comedy and *The Princess Casamassima* ends with a bang. But neither the marriage nor the suicide resolves the fundamental issues of the novels. Verena Tarrant is happy to be ransomed by Basil from the Bostonians, yet her happiness is a curiously mixed affair, and she departs in tears. The author-narrator notes, in the last sentence, that the denouement is neither comic nor happy: "It is to be feared that with the union, so far from brilliant, into which she was about to enter, these [tears] were not the last she was destined to shed."[22] Hyacinth Robinson's final act is also built upon ambiguities and many-sided social ties. He is unable to commit a crime against society, yet he cannot reject the appeal of his revolutionary comrades; the only target left is himself. Hyacinth's death is not a resolution—it is a despairing confession of the irresolvable complexities of his life.

The realists' opposition to neatly contrived resolutions and sentimental endings—those final group photographs of bright skies and smiling faces—was noted early by Charles Dudley Warner, who complained in the *Atlantic Monthly* that the realists believe "it is not artistic, and that it is untrue to nature to bring any novel to a definite consummation,

[22] *Century Magazine*, XXXI (February 1886), 600.   *Completion ↱ perfection*

and especially to end it happily.''[23] The answer to the *Atlantic* came from its former editor, now firmly and militantly seated in *Harper's* "Editor's Study": "[The novelist] must be true to what life has taught us is the truth, and after that he may let any fate betide his people; the novel ends well that ends faithfully.''[24] Henry James also replied to Warner and other critics in "The Art of Fiction," condemning novels which depend on "a 'happy ending,' on a distribution at the last of prizes, pensions, husbands, wives, babies, millions, appended paragraphs, and cheerful remarks.''[25] In the same essay, James took an amiable pot shot at Anthony Trollope, who had introduced the last chapter of *Barchester Towers* with a frank confession of his theory of fiction: "The end of a novel, like the end of a children's dinner-party, must be made up of sweetmeats and sugar-plums.''[26] James ridiculed the analogy between the ending of a novel and "that of a good dinner, a course of dessert and ices." Giving Trollope's figure another turn, James condemned those who regarded the artist in fiction as "a sort of meddlesome doctor who forbids agreeable aftertastes" (p. 506). Realistic cuisine, James might have added, is neither sweet nor bitter. It is a bittersweet mixture—a complex combination like that approved by Huck Finn, in which "things get mixed up, and the juice kind of swaps around, and the things go better."

[23] "Modern Fiction," LI (April 1883), 467.
[24] W. D. Howells, *Harper's Monthly*, LXXII (April 1886), 809.
[25] *Longman's Magazine*, IV (September 1884), 506.
[26] New York: Dodd, Mead & Co., 1901 (orig. pub. 1857), II, 344.

IRREGULAR SPHEROIDS

Realistic Characterization

REALISTIC fiction is deficient in prison intrigues, catacomb escapades, and moonlight melodrama. There is, as Howells noted, no murder, debauchery, arson, or pillage—not even a ghost or a shipwreck or a lady five thousand years old. The subdued plots of the realists negate narrative acrobatics; they affirm character. The realists were pragmatists who believed in an open, anthropocentric universe in which men might control their destinies. They believed that men acted on their environment, rather than simply reacting to it. They believed that character was superior to circumstance, and it was the commitment to character which resulted in the de-emphasis of incident in their writings.[1] In his Preface to *The Portrait of a Lady* James argued that "obviously the best thing in the book" was Isabel's long, actionless, meditative vigil in chapter 42. Isabel never utters a word; she never stirs from her chair in front of the dying fire. But Isabel's sedentary reflections, according to James, throw the action

---

[1] Some critics have traced the realists' de-emphasis of narrative action to an attempt to imitate the meandering mazes of "real life." James would have had little patience with such twentieth-century literary homeotherapy. "I saw clumsy Life again at her stupid work," he complained, recalling how a London dinner companion had given him his "grain of gold" for *The Spoils of Poynton* and then tarnished it by continuing with the confused and blundering denouement of actual event. "Real life" often provided James' vital particle, his germ, his sense of the subject, but only the intensity of the imagination and the discipline of art could mold it into fiction. See *The Art of the Novel*, ed. R. P. Blackmur (New York: Charles Scribner's Sons, 1934), pp. 120–121.

"further forward than twenty 'incidents' might have done."
They are "as 'interesting' as the surprise of a caravan or the
identification of a pirate."[2]

The realists prefer character analysis to gunfights off the
Barbary Coast, but they do not accept the seesaw theory of
plot and character in which one goes up as the other goes
down. Plot for the realists is inextricably linked to character;
narrative action is a result of character; people make events.
"What is character," asked James, "but the determination of
incident? What is incident but the illustration of character?
What is . . . a novel that is *not* of character? What else do
we seek in it and find in it?"[3] This is the burden of James'
prefaces to the New York Edition of his works, published
in 1907–9. In a rich variety of specific contexts, in relation
to some seventy of his productions, James hammered home
the realist's concept of character:

Trying to recover here, for recognition, the germ of my idea,
I see that it must have consisted not at all in any conceit of a
"plot," nefarious name, . . . but altogether in the sense of a
single character. . . .

I was myself so much more antecedently conscious of my
figures than of their setting. . . . I could think so little of any
situation that didn't depend for its interest on the nature of the
persons situated, and thereby on their way of taking it.

(Preface to *The Portrait of a Lady*)

For somehow . . . character, the question of what my agitated
friends should individually, and all intimately and at the core,
show themselves, would unmistakeably be the key to my modest
drama, and would indeed alone make a drama of any sort
possible.

(Preface to *The Spoils of Poynton*)[4]

2 *Art of the Novel*, p. 57.

3 "The Art of Fiction," *Longman's Magazine*, IV (September 1884),
512.

4 *Art of the Novel*, pp. 42, 44, 127. In the Preface to *The Portrait
of a Lady* (p. 43), James summarized his own views in a dramatized
reminiscence of the conversation of the "beautiful genius," Ivan
Turgenev: "I'm often accused of not having 'story' enough. I seem

James' prefaces also clarify the relationship between character and point of view. The emphasis on character is an essential basis for the realists' point of view, since the burden of narration—both in presentation and interpretation—is carried by the fictional characters, not by an omniscient author.

The novels of the mid-1880's are structured in terms of their leading characters, as even the titles reveal: *Adventures of Huckleberry Finn*, *The Princess Casamassima*, *The Rise of Silas Lapham*, *The Bostonians*, *The Minister's Charge; or, The Apprenticeship of Lemuel Barker*.[5] Each book focuses immediately on the main character, usually in the first sentence. Miss Pynsent of *The Princess Casamassima* opens that novel by stating, "Oh yes, I daresay I can find the child." The child is, of course, the book's protagonist, Hyacinth Robinson, who, as we discover five hundred pages later, is unable to find himself. In *The Bostonians* Basil Ransom is told in the first sentence that "Olive will come down in about ten minutes." (Olive does appear in about ten reading minutes, an interesting adherence to the unity of time which James, who can spin a thought out to a full chapter, is seldom at pains to observe.) In *Indian Summer* Theodore Colville is immediately presented lounging at the middle of the Ponte Vecchio in Florence. His reverie is soon broken by the appearance of a friend of his youth. Their greeting ("Mr. Colville!" "Why, Mrs. Bowen!") and their handclasp initiate an ironic comedy of manners in which, finally, the exclamations are removed from their greetings, the handclasp becomes an embrace, and

---

to myself to have as much as I need—to show my people, to exhibit their relations with each other; for that is all my measure."

[5] The significance of the realists' character-name titles becomes clear when their practice is contrasted with that of romantic writers. Hawthorne, for example, favors titles which indicate the place of the novel's action or its chief symbol; witness *The Scarlet Letter*, *The House of the Seven Gables*, *The Blithedale Romance*, and *The Marble Faun*.

Mrs. Bowen becomes Mrs. Colville. Silas Lapham opens his novel by calling out "Walk right in!" to Bartley Hubbard, a statement that also invites the reader. And in the best of all of these works, the leading character establishes himself at once in an arresting first sentence: "You don't know about me, without you have read a book by the name of 'The Adventures of Tom Sawyer,' but that ain't no matter." This immediate presentation of main fictional personages again demonstrates the close working relationship between character and point of view. If a character is to become the filter for the events of the book, that character has to be established before the narrative can begin in earnest.

Once the narrative has begun, the novels of James, Howells, and Twain demonstrate a consistent pattern of characterization. Each work places one or two perceptive characters in a complex social situation—which inevitably becomes a complex moral situation—to see what they will make of it. Huck confronts the entire Mississippi Valley, personified in the Widow Douglas and Miss Watson, Colonel Grangerford and old Baldy Shepherdson, the Duke and the King, Uncle Silas and Aunt Sally. Silas Lapham faces the perplexities of Boston. Olive Chancellor and Basil Ransom are set against each other. The results of these confrontations are not predictable, but they are always logically consistent with established elements of character.[6] They do not depend on external circumstances, implausible natural events, startling coincidences, and the other *di ex machinis* that stalk mechanically through much romantic fiction.

The realistic theory of characterization followed a middle course. At one extreme, it rejected eccentric, one-dimensional, idiosyncratic characters. Such caricatures are

---

[6] Twain overstates the case, but he captures the essential point in rule 11 of "Fenimore Cooper's Literary Offenses": "[Literary art requires] that the characters in a tale shall be so clearly defined that the reader can tell beforehand what each will do in a given emergency" (*North American Review*, CLXI [July 1895], 3).

often traced to Dickens, but the family is a large one, stemming ultimately from the humour characters of the Renaissance. Indigenous American examples include Hawthorne's Chillingworth, Edward Eggleston's Hoosiers, Bret Harte's reformed drunks and heart-of-gold prostitutes, and the "cigar-shop Indians" which Twain ridiculed as he tomahawked his way through "Fenimore Cooper's Literary Offenses."

At the opposite extreme, the realists opposed the ideal generic portraits defined both technically and aesthetically in a *Century* essay by John T. Stoddard concerning composite photography, a new process pioneered by Francis Galton. Illustrated with pictures of hollow-eyed, ghoulish composite college girls made by superimposing a number of negatives, Stoddard's article attempted to draw a moral for art:

We are all interested in typical representations. The novelist or poet holds and gratifies us as we feel that the character which is portrayed with skillful words is the type of a class. The artist draws an ideal head, his expression of a type for which no single model will serve, and we look with satisfaction and pleasure at the product of his fancy. Both artist and author seek to sketch a face or character that has grown in their minds by the blending of impressions gained from the observation of many individuals. The result at which they aim is a generic portrait which shall retain the typical characteristics of the class for which it stands, while the peculiarities and idiosyncrasies of the individuals are left out.[7]

Howells was probably not impressed by composite photography and certainly not by composite characterization. A few months later he dramatized the foolishness of Stoddard's artistic theory through the advice given the aspiring writer by a hypothetical literary pedant:

I see that you are looking at a grasshopper there which you have found in the grass, and I suppose you intend to describe it. Now

[7] *Century Magazine*, XXXIII (March 1887), 750.

don't waste your time and sin against culture in *that* way. I've got a grasshopper here, which has been evolved at considerable pains and expense out of the grasshopper in general; in fact, it's a type. It's made up of wire and card-board, very prettily painted in a conventional tint, and it's perfectly indestructible. It isn't very much like a real grasshopper, but it's a great deal nicer, and it's served to represent the notion of a grasshopper ever since man emerged from barbarism. You may say that it's artificial. Well, it *is* artificial; but then it's ideal too; and what you want to do is to cultivate the ideal.

Howells' irony was followed by a direct and vigorous statement of his faith in the average man who will have the courage to choose the "simple, honest, and natural grasshopper" and to reject the "ideal grasshopper, the heroic grasshopper, the impassioned grasshopper, the self-devoted, adventureful, good old romantic card-board grasshopper."[8]

Opposing both caricatures and generic portraits, the realists sought to strike a balance. Their characters became individualized without being eccentric, representative without being ideal. *The Rise of Silas Lapham* is a novel about the American businessman, but it is also a novel about a middle-aged ex-Vermonter who lives in Nankeen Square with his wife and daughters. Silas is an American businessman, but no other American businessman is quite like Silas. Olive Chancellor is a Boston reformer, not The Boston Reformer. Realistic characters are round rather than flat, but not too uniformly round as Howells noted in his description of Mrs. Leighton in *A Hazard of New Fortunes*: "She was not merely a prevailing mood, as people are apt to be in books, but was an irregularly spheroidal character, with

---

[8] "Editor's Study," *Harper's Magazine*, LXXVI (December 1887), 155. In James' "The Real Thing" the painter-narrator speaks for both himself and his creator: "I wanted to characterise closely, and the thing in the world I most hated was the danger of being ridden by a type" (*The Complete Tales of Henry James*, ed. Leon Edel [Philadelphia: J. B. Lippincott Co., 1962–64], VIII, 244).

surfaces that caught the different lights of circumstance and reflected them."[9]

Much of the irregularity of the spheroids of realistic fiction can be attributed to their complexity. Characters tend to have mixed motives and confused consciences, and they invariably discover that life is a complicated and ambiguous affair. All of the leading characters have devious and confused struggles with the perplexities of social and moral experience, usually culminating in key moments in the novels. Silas stays up all night attempting to resolve his financial difficulties—a night watch which his wife Persis compares to Jacob's wrestling with the angel. Silas, however, is ambiguously blessed ("*I* don't know what I am going to say to Rogers"), and he achieves a victory only by default. He delays his decision so long that it is no longer possible to swindle the Englishmen. Since Lapham's delay ruins his ex-partner Rogers, the rewards of honesty are obscure: Silas felt like a "thief and a murderer."

Howells' other characters also find themselves in perplexing situations. The Reverend David Sewell of *The Minister's Charge* both accepts and rejects his position as adviser to Lemuel Barker, his accidentally acquired charge. Lemuel himself is simultaneously in and out of love with Statira; his predicament at the end of the novel epitomizes the realistic sensibility: "There were instants when he knew himself guiltless of all the wrong of which in another sense he knew himself guilty."[10] In *Indian Summer* Theodore Colville discovers that he aspires to disaster, that his greatest mistake would be to achieve what he thought he wanted most. The unbalanced triangle is resolved when forty-one-year-old Colville abandons his impossible visions of spring

<hr/>

[9] *Harper's Weekly*, XXXIII (18 May 1889), 385. The concept of "round" and "flat" characters was popularized by E. M. Forster in *Aspects of the Novel* (New York: Harcourt, Brace & Co., 1927), pp. 103–118.

[10] *Century Magazine*, XXXII (October 1886), 892.

and gives up his pursuit of beautiful twenty-year-old Imogene Graham. Colville finally learns that the autumnal mildness of Indian summer can be a dangerous fraud. The novel's title is ironic, as is *The Rise* (fall) *of Silas Lapham* and *The Apprenticeship of Lemuel Barker* (the Reverend David Sewell). Perhaps Howells is hinting at that derivation of Indian summer which claims that the season "afforded the Indians another opportunity of visiting the settlements with their destructive warfare."[11] But Howells' irony, characteristically, comes full circle. Indian summer *can* be a pleasant season, if one has no illusions. Lemuel Barker *does* serve an apprenticeship. Silas Lapham *does* rise, morally, out of the ashes of his financial ruin.

The triangle in *The Bostonians* is lopsided as well as unbalanced, since Olive Chancellor competes with Basil Ransom for the affections of Verena Tarrant. James is never coarse, or even obvious, but he relentlessly investigates the homosexual ties that bind Olive to Verena. Aberrant sexuality is not Olive's only problem, for she also has a complex schism in her attitude toward reform. She violently throws her lot in with the poor and oppressed, yet, at bottom, she deplores their lack of taste and refinement. Olive loathes the crowded horse-drawn streetcars of Boston, but she resolutely rides them in order to mingle in the common life. Like Dante's sinners, she trembles at the threshold, immobilized by simultaneous attraction and repulsion. But James takes it a circle deeper. Olive not only hates the

---

[11] Philip Doddridge, "Notes on the Indian Wars" (1824); quoted by H. L. Mencken, *The American Language: Supplement I* (New York: Alfred A. Knopf, 1945), pp. 182–183.

Emily Dickinson was not thinking of Indian attacks, but she too was aware of the treacheries of the season:

> These are the days when skies resume
> The old—old sophistries of June—
> A blue and gold mistake.

("These are the days when Birds come back," no. 130, *The Complete Poems of Emily Dickinson*, ed. Thomas H. Johnson [Boston: Little, Brown & Co., 1960], p. 61.)

plebeians she professes to love, she loves them because she hates them—thus whetting the inward-turned knife of martyrdom.

Realistic characters are composed of a mixture of virtues and defects, selflessness and selfishness; they exhibit what Howells called the "God-given complexity of motive which we find in all the human beings we know."[12] Realistic fiction is searched in vain for impossibly courageous or totally corrupt men, or for faultless blonde women—the Priscilla-Phoebe-Hilda syndrome which has a delicate stranglehold on much of Hawthorne's fiction. There are no angels or devils, heroes or villains. Even the debased characters of the mid-1880's—the Duke and the King, Olive Chancellor, Rogers, Selah Tarrant—are humanly pathetic rather than superhumanly evil. There are no diabolical Claggarts, no Fedallahs, no Chillingworths with eyes lit by fires of hell. Instead we have the King, whose bloodshot eyes reflect only gastric flames.

The realists' complexity of characterization extends to groups as well as to individuals. In *The Princess Casamassima* the reader is led to probe the multiple levels of revolution through the wide-ranging variety of revolutionaries James presents. We see the shadowy foreign conspirator (Hoffendahl), the sincere but condescendingly dabbling aristocrat (the Princess), the progressive young laborite (Paul Muniment), the fiery but ineffectual French exile (M. Poupin), the altruistic social worker (Lady Aurora), the old, disenchanted reformer who has given up on the world and its problems (Mr. Vetch), the beery table pounders (at the "Sun and Moon"), and the thoroughly mixed up young man, Hyacinth Robinson, whose sympathies are as confused as the nationality and social status of his parents—an English nobleman and a French prostitute. It is no wonder that Hyacinth shoots himself—a victim, like Henry Adams, of historical multiplicity. But James doesn't stop there. In order

[12] "Editor's Study," *Harper's Monthly*, LXXII (May 1886), 972.

to provide the full social dimension, he creates a control group of nonrevolutionaries: the timid seamstress (Miss Pynsent), the hypocritical captain who lets the revolutionaries amuse him (Sholto), the reactionary (Prince Casamassima), and that blooming personification of cockney London, Millicent Henning.

In *The Minister's Charge* Howells creates a similar if less revolutionary social panorama with a Boston minister (David Sewell), a Brahmin (Bromfield Corey), an ex-convict ("Williams"), the working girls (Statira and 'Manda), the nonworking girls (Miss Swan and Miss Carver), the bourgeois hotelkeeper (Mrs. Harmon), and the explosive Irish handy man (Jerry). The apprenticeship of Lemuel Barker (the book's subtitle) is economic and social, an initiation in which Barker's success is based on his ever-enlarging knowledge of Boston's class structure. His involvement in and perception of complex social distinctions result in the rise of Lemuel Barker, while similar involvements and perceptions cause the downfall and eventual suicide of Hyacinth Robinson.

Hyacinth discovers, in despair, that the world is a more complicated place than he had thought. Although Hyacinth's startling fate is unusual in a realistic novel, his dilemma is not; for the confrontation of a complex character with the ambiguities of experience provides the premise for the realistic fiction of the eighties. This premise was summarized by James in his Preface to *The Princess Casamassima*. Realistic characters must be intelligent ("the power to be finely aware and richly responsible"), yet they must be bewildered ("without which there would be no question of an issue or of the fact of suspense"). The story lies in the character's formulation of his bewilderment: "The interest of the attitude and the act would be the actor's imagination and vision of them."[13] James' discussion of character thus reaches

[13] *Art of the Novel*, pp. 62–64.

113

out to embrace the perplexity of human experience and the perception and presentation of that perplexity. These three elements—character, complexity, point of view—form a tightly woven triangle which is the figure in the carpet of realistic fiction.

CHAPTER VIII

PERPETUAL FIGURES

The Uses of Imagery

IN 1879 Henry James was thirty-six years old. The author of four novels and three dozen tales, he was on the threshold of his full career and of the realism that was to flower so remarkably in the decade of the 1880's. "Daisy Miller," that "outrage on American girlhood," was causing a satisfying international stir; *Washington Square* was under way; the first outlines of Isabel Archer had been sketched in James' notebook.

James paused on this threshold to survey the American literary past in his short biography of Hawthorne written for John Morley's English Men of Letters Series. The book is curiously mixed. James was respectful, even a little proud of his predecessor: Hawthorne was the "most eminent representative of a literature"; he was "the most valuable example of the American genius." Hawthorne, after all, was the only American to be designated an English Man of Letters. Nevertheless, James' praise was always qualified. Although Hawthorne was the most eminent representative of American literature, "the importance of the literature may be questioned." Hawthorne represented the American genius, but "that genius has not, as a whole, been literary." Hawthorne might confidently be selected as the American who had most "enriched the mother tongue," yet his stature was relative: "There is something very fortunate for him in the way that he borrows an added relief from the absence of competitors in his own line, and from the general flatness of the literary field that surrounds him."[1]

[1] Henry James, *Hawthorne* (New York: Harper & Bros., 1879), p. 2.

Written at a time when James was just coming into full possession of his talent, his critical sketch of Hawthorne reveals more about him than Hawthorne, more about realism than romanticism. James repeatedly turned to the problem, as he saw it, of Hawthorne's allegorical and symbolic method. He found *The Scarlet Letter* burdened with "a certain superficial symbolism. . . . It is overdone at times, and becomes mechanical" (pp. 114, 117). The allegorical technique of "Ethan Brand" and other tales struck James as

quite one of the lighter exercises of the imagination. Many excellent judges, I know, have a great stomach for it; they delight in symbols and correspondences, in seeing a story told as if it were another and a very different story. I frankly confess that I have as a general thing but little enjoyment of it and that it has never seemed to me to be, as it were, a first-rate literary form.
[pp. 62–63]

James' objections to the creaky machinery of the allegorical method and the highflying symbols of romantic fiction are another manifestation of the realists' antiomniscience. They were suspicious of the symbolic mode because the symbol is often a leap into the supernatural, the spiritual, the transcendental; it may invoke a meaning which is independent of the work at hand. Carlyle, in arguing for symbolism in *Sartor Resartus*, summarized the realists' objections: "In the Symbol proper . . . there is, more or less distinctly and directly, some embodiment and revelation of the Infinite; the Infinite is made to blend itself with the Finite, to stand visible, and as it were, attainable there."[2]

The transcendental nature of symbolism—its linking of finite and infinite, human and divine (or demonic)—makes it a primary technique for writers who affirm the reality of a spiritual realm. The intense faith of the Puritans had planted the symbolic tradition early and deeply in American soil.

[2] *Sartor Resartus, The Works of Thomas Carlyle* (London: Chapman & Hall, 1896), I, 175 (bk. III, ch. 3).

The analogies of Special Providence alleged that God's footprints could be read, that every physical act proved a general theological point: "For Diñ[n]er, very good Rost Lamb, Turkey, Fowls, Aplepy [apple pie]. After Diñer, sung the 121 Psalm. Note. A Glass of spirits my Wife sent stood upon a Joint-Stool which, Simon W. jogging, it fell down and broke all to shivers: I said twas a lively Emblem of our Fragility and Mortality."[3] Hawthorne refused to worship at the iron altar of Calvinism, but like the Puritans he created a world that bristled with symbols, types, and emblems. Melville believed that "some certain significance lurks in all things," that nature and man's soul are joined by "linked analogies." Whitman proclaimed himself to be a "uniter of here and hereafter, / Taking all hints . . . but swiftly leaping beyond them." Emerson spoke for a well-established tradition when he proposed, in *Nature*, that "every natural fact is a symbol of some spiritual fact."[4]

The realists' doubts about spiritual facts, the existence of the soul, and the accessibility of the infinite led them to reject the symbolic tradition, a rejection well illustrated in Charles Feidelson's *Symbolism and American Literature*.[5] Feidelson has separate sections dealing with Hawthorne, Whitman, Melville, Poe, Emerson, Thoreau, and "modern [twentieth-century] literature"—none on the realists. In his index Melville is alloted sixty-five lines, Emerson thirty-one, and Hawthorne twenty-two. Howells and Mark Twain are not mentioned; James rates a single line. The American literature omitted by Feidelson is that of the realists, who

3 *Diary of Samuel Sewall*, Collections of the Massachusetts Historical Society, 5th series, V (Boston, 1878), 460.

4 *Moby-Dick*, ed. Charles Feidelson, Jr. (Indianapolis: Bobbs-Merrill Co., 1964), pp. 406, 549; "Out of the Cradle Endlessly Rocking," lines 20–21, *Leaves of Grass* (Comprehensive Reader's Edition), ed. Harold W. Blodgett and Sculley Bradley (New York: New York University Press, 1965), p. 247; *Nature*, in *Selections from Ralph Waldo Emerson*, ed. Stephen E. Whicher (Boston: Houghton Mifflin Co., 1957), p. 32.

5 Chicago: University of Chicago Press, 1953.

turned, as Harry Levin says of the medieval separation of secularized West from orthodox East, "from the symbolic, in short, to the representational."[6]

Although it is not primarily symbolic, realistic fiction of the 1880's is highly figurative. For the realists, as for Dexter Freer and his wife, impressions continually refer "to other impressions, because they had the key to almost everything that needed an answer—because, in a word, they were able to compare."[7] The realists rely on short-range, mundane comparisons instead of long-range horizon-leaping symbolic analogies. Their reference is horizontal, rather than vertical, and it consists largely of similes and metaphors. The outward-moving symbols of the romantics sought a correspondence between earthly existence and divine or devilish worlds, or generalized from the actions of individual men to the universal experience of man. Realistic imagery compares experiences to other concrete experiences, a technique which restricts the dimensions of the fictive world to those of ordinary human existence.

This specific density contrasts sharply with the practice of romantic authors. Arthur Dimmesdale's shriek in the night reverberates "as if a company of devils" had seized upon it. Chillingworth's eyes burn with the hell-fire of "Bunyan's awful doorway." The *Pequod* submerges in a tide of expansive similes: "as Turkish mutes bowstring their victim"; "as in the gaseous Fata Morgana"; "like Satan"; "as it rolled five thousand years ago."[8] Romantic imagery tends to enlarge the field of vision; realistic imagery sharpens the focus.

[6] "What Is Realism?" *Contexts of Criticism* (New York: Atheneum, 1963), p. 70.

[7] Henry James, "Lady Barberina" (1884), *The Complete Tales of Henry James*, ed. Leon Edel (Philadelphia: J. B. Lippincott Co., 1962–64), V, 196.

[8] Nathaniel Hawthorne, *The Scarlet Letter*, ed. Larzer Ziff (text of the Centenary Edition; Indianapolis: Bobbs-Merrill Co., 1963), pp. 124, 142; *Moby-Dick*, pp. 721–723.

Realistic imagery is specific, concrete, and mundane. The Reverend Mr. Sewell shakes the hand of rural Mrs. Barker and finds that "it felt like a collection of corn-cobs." Silas Lapham's ex-partner Rogers speaks in a tone which has "the flat succinct sound of two pieces of wood clapped together." Olive Chancellor looks forward to suffering, "for the prospect of suffering was always, spiritually speaking, so much cash in her pocket." Huck finds that the elaborate rituals of Tom Sawyer's robber gang aren't worth a "mouthful of ashes." Colonel Sherburn's laugh is "not the pleasant kind, but the kind that makes you feel like when you are eating bread that's got sand in it."

The particularity of realistic imagery serves Henry James especially well. James' style, like Montaigne's, is a "perpetual figure, renewed at every step. . . . Thought and image, with him, it is all one."[9] James' metaphors dramatize his abstractions; they provide solidity of specification. James is especially adept at portraying states of mind, often highly complex ones, with a vivid imagistic snap. In *The Princess Casamassima* Miss Pynsent's rosy picture of the future is destroyed by Mrs. Bowerbank: "It struck her that Mrs. Bowerbank's heavy hand had suddenly punched a hole in the canvas." Hyacinth admires the intellectual dexterity of the Princess: "the movement—his eyes seemed to see it—with which in any direction, intellectually, she could fling open her windows." Mrs. Tarrant's flaccid subordination and her leaden mind are made metaphorically tangible in *The Bostonians*: "Her husband's tastes rubbed off on her soft, moist moral surface"; she is a "non-conductor" of her daughter's intellect. James relies on this sort of imagery throughout his long career. In many respects it makes possible his psychological complexities by imaginatively converting them to reality, a reality that is only analogous, but one which is solid to the hand and visible to the eye.

[9] C. A. Sainte-Beuve, *Port-Royal*, II, 443–444; quoted and translated by Donald M. Frame, *The Complete Works of Montaigne* (Stanford, Calif.: Stanford University Press, 1957), p. vii.

The realists use imagery for extended patterns as well as individual effects. Recurring, related metaphors are often used to define character. Olive Chancellor's inflexibility and her lack of femininity are expressed in images of ice and adamant. Her smile "might have been likened to a thin ray of moonlight resting upon the wall of a prison." Her eyes contain the "glitter of green ice." She gives the impression of "feeling cold," of "bristling with steel." The other Boston reformers are also hanged in metaphorical effigy. Miss Birdseye's platform-weary face suggests the "reflection of ugly lecture-lamps." She talks inanely, incessantly, "in a voice of which the spring seemed broken, like that of an over-worked bell-wire." Selah Tarrant is a coarse and greedy mesmerist, a sensual spiritualist, whose "slow, deliberate smile, which made his mouth enormous, developed two wrinkles, as long as the wings of a bat . . . and showed a set of big, even, carnivorous teeth."

Huck Finn is a vernacular virtuoso who commands a wide range of imagery. He makes the reader look freshly at common things by renaming them so they take on the coloration of his point of view. Lies are "stretchers" or facts "painted up considerable"; Miss Watson wears "goggles"; the clock strikes "twelve licks"; girls "brisken up" their rooms with "jimcracks"; the King's eulogy is "soul-butter and hogwash"; a stranger in Pikesville "lays over the yaller fever, for interest." Huck is an expert at using old language in new places and in new ways: "I catched a cat-fish and haggled him open with my knife"; "it looked late and *smelt* late"; Mary Jane Wilks "had more sand in her than any girl I ever see." And he constantly converts adjectives and verbs into metaphors: "There was freckled places on the ground where the light sifted down through the leaves"; "Towards night it begun to darken up and look like rain; the heat lightning was squirting around, low down in the sky, and the leaves was beginning to shiver." Huck's highly figurative language—a kind of colloquial poetry—is one of the main supports for the point of view which Twain establishes so successfully in the novel.

The particularity of realistic comparisons tends to break down the division between the subject and the object to which it is compared. Analogy approaches reality; metaphor becomes meaning—a complex fact of language and psychology that the realists use to advantage. Huck's description of Pap—"His hair was long and tangled and greasy, and hung down, and you could see his eyes shining through like he was behind vines"—isolates him forever from human society. Pap is a creature of the jungle. Huck's metaphors for the color of his face—"a tree-toad white, a fish-belly white"—give Pap a coating of cold slime that never rubs off. Neither Huck nor the reader wastes any tears when Jim reveals that Pap is dead. James' images also tend to break down the separation between, in I. A. Richards' terms, the tenor and the vehicle of a metaphor.[10] Miss Birdseye's head looked "as if it had been soaked, blurred, and made vague by exposure to some slow dissolvent." This is only *as if*, yet the mind leaps lightly over the connective.[11] *As if* becomes *is*. Miss Birdseye's features and her vague doctrines never recover from their metaphorical dissolution. The ice images

[10] *The Philosophy of Rhetoric* (New York: Oxford University Press, 1936), pp. 96 ff. The tenor is the "principal subject"; the vehicle is "what it resembles."

[11] The connotative force of a word or phrase is often stronger than its denotative value and can even reverse the meaning of a sentence. Mark Twain attempted to build a punch-line apology into his parody of Longfellow, Emerson, and Holmes at the *Atlantic Monthly* birthday dinner for Whittier in 1877: "Why, my dear sir, *these* were not the gracious singers to whom we and the world pay loving reverence and homage; these were impostors." The artificiality of "gracious singers" and "loving reverence" combined with the force of "impostors" to effectively erase the "not." Twain was left with a direct insult hanging heavily in the silent and smoky air at the Hotel Brunswick. The speech was originally published in the Boston *Evening Transcript*, 18 December 1877, and reprinted in *Mark Twain's Speeches*, introd. W. D. Howells (New York: Harper & Bros., 1910), pp. 1–7.

which surround Olive Chancellor convince the reader that she would be cold to the touch. Selah Tarrant's "big, even, carnivorous teeth" reduce him to animal status—a flesh-eating spiritualist who even preys on his family.

The realistic fiction of the mid-1880's is not symbolic in the traditional sense, but it does employ symbols. The realists deny the transcendental symbolic imagination which ascends from natural facts to spiritual facts, but they do use tightly reined internal symbols, which—like realistic morals—are built into the fabric of the narrative and do not depend on external values for their meaning.[12] Natural facts, for the realists, are symbols of other natural facts.

The symbols of the realists, like their similes and metaphors, are largely devoted to the revelation of character. In *Indian Summer*, Mrs. Bowen's jealousy is caught in the firelight which "flickered upon her face, and threw upon the ceiling a writhing, fantastic shadow, the odious caricature of her gentle beauty." Miss Birdseye, an ineffective, incoherent reformer in *The Bostonians*, is symbolized by her displaced spectacles, a literal natural fact that James borrowed from Elizabeth Peabody.[13] Olive's futile attempt to possess Verena, Basil's eventual victory in separating them, and the ironic fact that Olive first invited Basil to Boston and introduced him to Verena are all captured in James' symbolic

[12] In a discussion of *A Modern Instance* Edwin H. Cady notes that Howells' symbols "have no referents outside the immediate field of the novel. They do not point to abstractions of general validity or significance. They function only to give heightened imaginative power to the particular work" (*The Road to Realism* [Syracuse: Syracuse University Press, 1956], p. 214).

[13] James argued with his brother William concerning his use of Miss Peabody (who lived until 1894), and he admitted having a "scruple" about the spectacles. See *The Notebooks of Henry James*, ed. F. O. Matthiessen and Kenneth B. Murdock (New York: Oxford University Press, 1947), pp. 67–68. James also uses the spectacles to symbolize the incoherence of the entire reform movement: "The whole moral history of Boston was reflected in her displaced spectacles."

stage directions: "Olive put out her hands to hold her, and at this moment one of the *portières* of the room was pushed aside, while a gentleman was ushered in by Miss Chancellor's little parlour-maid." Silas Lapham is fascinated by the symbolic pile driver (a magnification of Silas' great, hairy, pounding fist) which slams home the foundation of his new house: "By gracious! . . . there ain't anything like that in *this* world for *business.*"

Lapham's house is in many ways the symbolic center of the novel. Built on the "New Land" on the water side of Boston's Beacon Street, the hundred-thousand-dollar triumph represents the apex of Lapham's financial trajectory.[14] The house is tangible proof that Silas is indeed a "Solid Man of Boston," but the foundation is unsound. The house is a symbol of Lapham's social pretensions and his ruthless extermination of his partner. "There's blood on it," Mrs. Lapham protests; "I shan't live in it." Even the architectural rise which the house represents is superficial: the architect has to maneuver skillfully to circumvent the gauche tastes of the family from Lumberville and Nankeen Square. It is appropriate—even inevitable—that Lapham himself should be responsible for the destruction of the new house; his expired insurance policy provides the final ironic twist.

The Beacon Street fire which warms a curious crowd ("Isn't it perfectly magnificent! . . . I wouldn't have missed it on any account") not only destroys Lapham's multifarious aspirations. It also consumes the money which could have rescued the faltering paint business and puts Silas in the hands of his creditors. The destruction of the house is an

---

[14] Howells at the time was engaged in a move to Beacon Street. "Drolly enough," he wrote to James in August, 1884, "I am writing a story in which the chief personage builds a house 'on the water side of Beacon,' and I shall be able to use all my experience, down to the quick. Perhaps the novel may pay for the house" (*Life in Letters of William Dean Howells*, ed. Mildred Howells [Garden City, N. Y.: Doubleday, Doran & Co., 1928], I, 366).

integral, functional symbol. It represents Lapham's collapse and, in turn, is a partial cause of that collapse. Appropriately, the smoke-stained shell has the last figurative word: "The windows looked like the eye-sockets of a skull down upon the blackened and trampled snow of the street."

The architectural symbolism in *The Rise of Silas Lapham* is a logical corollary of realistic subject matter. In his concern for ordinary people in their everyday lives Howells puts a strong emphasis on their houses. Ordinary people spend more than half of their everyday lives in their houses, and much of their energy is invested in building, repairing, furnishing, and feathering their nests. The symbolic qualities are irresistible—the house becomes the man. Lapham's Vermont farmhouse represents both his rural origins and his subsequent graceless prosperity. The original ugliness has been "smartened up with a coat of Lapham's own paint, and heightened with an incongruous piazza." The house in Nankeen Square is a monument to expensively indulged bad taste—a medley of green and salmon paint surrounding gray and red velvet wallpaper and gilt molding, topped by a chandelier of "massive imitation bronze." For decoration the Laphams selected allegorical statues of faith and prayer and "a white marble group of several figures, expressing an Italian conception of Lincoln Freeing the Slaves—a Latin Negro and his wife—with our Eagle flapping his wings in approval, at Lincoln's feet."

The rural equivalent of the Lapham drawing room is the Grangerford parlor in *Adventures of Huckleberry Finn*, full of gaudy plaster parrots, crockery cats and dogs, wild-turkey-wing fans, and "a lovely crockery basket that had apples and oranges and peaches and grapes piled up in it which was much redder and yellower and prettier than real ones is, but they warn't real because you could see where pieces had got chipped off and showed the white chalk or whatever it was, underneath" (p. 137). James also relies on the symbolism of architecture and interior decoration. Olive's narrow parlor, Miss Birdseye's bleak, empty meeting room, and the Tarrants' cottage in Cambridge all express the character of their owners in *The Bostonians*. A major shift in the plot of *The Princess Casamassima* is signaled when the Princess moves from under the "high-piled ancient russet roof" of her massive *casa* to a small, bare house in a meager London district: "When thousands and tens of thousands haven't bread to put in their mouths I can dispense with tapestry and old china." The novel's countercurrent is revealed when Hyacinth—whose revolutionary sympathies are a product of the shabby boardinghouse in Lomax Place—develops an increasing admiration for the country houses of the rich. The social panorama of the novel is revealed in the juxtaposition of houses, just as all of Boston is momentarily brought into focus by Miss Kingsbury in *The Rise of Silas Lapham*: "I have often thought of our great, cool houses standing useless here, and the thousands of poor creatures stifling in their holes and dens, and the little children dying for wholesome shelter."

Even the pine shavings from Lapham's new house have a symbolic value in the scene in which Irene Lapham sits on a sawhorse with Tom Corey and pokes at a shaving with her parasol. Ever since George Arms suggested that the scene had an "undertone of sexual symbolism"[15] it has been difficult to read it any other way:

"You seem to have a great passion for playing with shavings," he said. "Is it a new one?"

"New what?"

"Passion."

"I don't know," she said, dropping her eyelids, and keeping on with her effort. She looked shyly aslant at him. "Perhaps you don't approve of playing with shavings?"

"Oh yes, I do. I admire it very much. But it seems rather difficult. I've a great ambition to put my foot on the shaving's tail and hold it for you."

"Well," said the girl.

[15] Introduction, *The Rise of Silas Lapham* (New York: Holt, Rinehart & Winston, 1949), p. xiii.

"Thank you," said the young man. He did so, and now she ran her parasol point easily through it. They looked at each other and laughed. "That was wonderful. Would you like to try another?" he asked.

"No, I thank you," she replied. "I think one will do."[16]

"What do you suppose he meant by it," Irene asks her sister—a question now shared by the reader. Given Howells' taste, if not his reticence, and given the nature of the *Century Magazine* audience in 1885, the scene cannot be overt sexual symbolism. When Silas merely pointed out to Corey the place in the unfinished house where the girls' room was to be, "it seemed terribly intimate. Irene blushed deeply and turned her head away." There are other problems. Irene, not Tom, is the parasol provocateur and, at that, Irene is the wrong sister: Tom is in love with Penelope. The Freudian response is predictable—a question of role reversal, sublimation, and Howellsian repressions unconsciously bubbling up to the surface. Perhaps, but Howells himself explains the scene in a later passage. Sensible Penelope tells her sister that she was playing with shavings "to hide your embarrassment." It is an adroit symbol of the adolescent social unease which finds a variety of expressions in toe scuffing, tie straightening, button twisting and cigarette puffing.

The nature of Tom's participation should not be overlooked in the scramble for sexual interpretations. Tom has little interest in Irene, yet he endures her ignorance (giving her a reading list as they share the sawhorse) and joins in her embarrassed trifling because he is a gentleman. The Laphams cannot understand a man who is polite to ladies simply for the sake of politeness. This misunderstanding is an important reflection of the Laphams' naïveté, and it establishes the narrative subplot—the Laphams' mistaken notion that Tom is courting beautiful Irene rather than witty Penelope. The triviality of the pine shaving on which Irene builds her romantic castle (she ties it elaborately with a ribbon and

16 *Century Magazine,* XXIX (February 1885), p. 584.

cherishes it as a keepsake) underscores the fatuity of her affection. The shaving thus carries a good deal of internal symbolic meaning. Its sexual significance depends, ultimately, on the reader. Like many would-be Freudian symbols, the shaving remains a Rorschach blot.

Realistic symbols are intrinsic, specific, localized—characteristics clarified by contrasting the fall of the house of Lapham with the preternatural collapse of the mysterious house of Usher. The realists also attempt to internalize their symbolism by using traditional symbols in an unusual or ironic manner, thus snapping their chains of association. The allegorical rose which grows in countless literary gardens (including the grassplot in front of the prison house in *The Scarlet Letter*, serving, "let us hope, to symbolize some sweet moral blossom") is plucked and withered by realistic irony. The uselessness of Miss Vane's charity in *The Minister's Charge* is astringently symbolized by the Jacqueminot rosebud which she bestows on a Chinaman dying of cancer.[17] There are no expanding circles of moral sweetness. In *The Bostonians* Olive Chancellor employs hackneyed symbols to describe her role in the coming feminist revolution: "The names of those who had helped to show the way and lead

---

[17] Miss Vane's name and those of Miss Pynsent (a seamstress), Basil Ransom (who rescues Verena), and spiritually myopic Miss Birdseye suggest that in name symbolism, at least, the realists are not so subtle. Generally, however, realistic names tend toward implication rather than allegory. Silas has an unspecified bucolic tone, and Lumberville is an appropriate origin for the Laphams. Their home in Nankeen Square, like the cloth (and the Laphams themselves), is durable but tasteless. The realists also enjoy historical and etymological derivations. The derelict steamboat in *Huckleberry Finn* is the *Walter Scott*. Olive Chancellor's name hints at "keeper" and the Southern Civil War victory at Chancellorsville—an ironic foreshadowing of Olive's defeat by Basil (a Mississippian). Howells enjoys naming Bromfield's ancestor Giles Corey, who was pressed to death for witchcraft. Persis Lapham is perhaps a glance at her simplistic persistence. Amariah Farrinder suggests pariah. "Medley," the Princess' estate, captures the mixture of her social inclinations.

the squadrons would be the brightest in the tables of fame." These are successful precisely because they are hackneyed. The symbols do not work; Olive fools only herself.

The Minister's Charge contains an entire chapter based on the symbol of a ray of light. Despairing and lonely, Lemuel Barker wanders toward Mr. Sewell's house. He is cheered by the light that "streamed bright and strong from the drawing-room window" and eagerly rings the bell:

"Oh—Mr. Barker! Come in! Come in! . . . How in the world did you happen to come?"

"I was passing and saw the light. . . ."

"To be sure! We never have any idea how far our little candle throws its beams!"

But Mr. Sewell's reluctant hospitality and his shallow sympathy soon become apparent to Lemuel and he is unable to disclose his grief:

"Is there anything—something—you wished to speak with me about?"

"No. No, not anything in particular. I just saw the light, and—"

"It was so good of you to run in and see me. Don't fancy it's been any disturbance. I'd got into rather a dim place in my work, but since I've been standing here with you—ha, ha, ha! those things do happen so curiously!—the whole thing has become perfectly luminous. . . . Glad of this moment with you, if it's *only* a moment! Goodbye!"[18]

Shut out once more in the night, Lemuel muses over the "dim place [that] had not become so luminous to him as it had to the minister" and the "false lights of feeble-hearted pity." In this crucial moment in the novel the minister betrays his charge. The ray of light that streams from his window is, finally, a light that failed.

The light that failed for the realists was the light of omniscience, of transcendentalism, of shining worlds above. Left to their own resources both philosophically and artis-

[18] *Century Magazine,* XXXIII (November 1886), 41.

tically, the realists turned to antiomniscient narrative presentation, to the use of ambiguity and complex ironies, to character. These elements are linked and strengthened by realistic imagery, which, stripped of external sources of meaning and intrinsically relevant to the narrative, is a key source of internal illumination.

THE LITERARY CONTEXT

CHAPTER IX

REALISM AND
AMERICAN LITERARY HISTORY

IF THE preceding study of realism has been successful, it should now be possible to consider the movement in a larger context. The perspectives of literary history help to define and clarify realism, just as realism provides a vantage point from which certain questions of literary history may be freshly evaluated. Is realism flatly opposed to romanticism? Is local color writing "realistic"? Are realism and naturalism parts of the same general movement, as Professors Becker and Berthoff suggest? Is Richard Poirier justified in leap-frogging over (and through) the realists to find the romantic visionary power which he feels is the true antecedent of the best twentieth-century writing? What is the debt which modern writers owe to the realists? Is realism a bold new note of the second half of the nineteenth century or simply another echo of Victorian gentility, soon to be swept away by the vigorous literary generation which came to maturity in the 1890's? Did the realists win or lose the "realism war"?

As we have seen, the realists rejected many aspects of romantic belief and technique: exotic subjects, idealism, omniscience, narrative convulsions and coincidences, neatly resolved endings, transcendental symbolism. Yet it is a mistake to simplistically oppose realism to romanticism, and it is unhistorical. Howells praised Emerson's recognition of the worth of the common, the familiar, the usual—"banks and tariffs, the newspaper and caucus, Methodism and Unitarianism."[1] All the realists agreed with Emerson's dictum

---

[1] "Editor's Study," *Harper's Monthly*, LXXV (October 1887), 803.

not to seek outside the self.[2] Henry James was too intelligent an artist not to profit by both the successes and the limitations of his predecessors. In spite of his condescension James commends Hawthorne's "genuine democratic feeling" and his "relish for the commoner stuff of human nature." He is enthusiastic over what he considers Hawthorne's greatest strength—"he cared for the deeper psychology."[3] This is, of course, James' own strength, and it indicates an important similarity between American romantic and realistic writers.

The Scarlet Letter illustrates both similarities and differences. Hawthorne's novel is told by an omniscient author-narrator who is able to see around trees and into the souls of his characters. He steps forward to judge his puppets and make historical comparisons between the coarse "wives and maidens of old English birth" and their "fair descendants." Nevertheless, this omniscience is qualified by several dramatic scenes—in the forest, on the scaffolding, in Dimmesdale's study—and by the occasional tendency of the author-narrator to adopt the attitudes of the Puritans. Bleak descriptions ("sad-colored garments," "iron spikes," "a yet darker aspect of its beetle-browed and gloomy front") and archaic language ("mistress," "hath," "wottest," "betimes," "eldritch") support the credibility of a narrator who can state, seriously and straightforwardly, that Mistress Hibbins "was well known to make excursions into the forest" with "fiends and night-hags."[4] This point of view provides

---

[2] "Ne te quaesiveris extra," prefatory epigraph to "Self-Reliance," *Selections from Ralph Waldo Emerson*, ed. Stephen E. Whicher (Boston: Houghton Mifflin Co., 1957), p. 147. The realists' denial of the Over-Soul extended their self-reliance beyond Emerson's. They would have rewritten his famous conclusion to "Give All to Love":

> Heartily know,
> When half-gods go,
> Man arrives.

[3] Henry James, *Hawthorne* (New York: Harper & Bros., 1879), pp. 47, 65.

[4] Nathaniel Hawthorne, *The Scarlet Letter*, ed. Larzer Ziff (text of the Centenary Edition; Indianapolis: Bobbs-Merrill Co., 1963), p. 142.

one framework of judgment for Hester's crime and enables Hawthorne to present part of his story in terms of the Massachusetts Bay Puritans of 1641. At times, the author-narrator of *The Scarlet Letter* is a grim, bearded man of iron —a central consciousness complete with Bible and sword.

The realists found Hawthorne's fiction too obvious. A concluding chapter entitled "Conclusion" and a stated moral ("Be true! Be true!") were antithetic to the realists' illusion of objectivity and their concern for the complexities of experience.[5] Yet Hawthorne was able to create complexity through such means as the ambiguity of the alternative choice: Did Dimmesdale have a scarlet letter? Did he cut it himself? Did Chillingworth cause it to appear? Was it psychosomatic? Presumably the reader is left to choose for himself, but often the effect is cumulative—all of the possibilities remain. This structural complexity is related to realistic practice, yet it differs in that Hawthorne's ambiguity enables him to tiptoe along the edge of the supernatural. The realists rejected the supernatural, but they recognized a kinship to the moral complexity of *The Scarlet Letter*, in which all the characters are ultimately right and wrong, sinned against and sinning. The act of adultery is wrong, but it does have its sanctity. Chillingworth is a monster, yet the reader is softened by the description of the former days in which he basked in the warm light of Hester's nuptial smile after having given his best years "to feed the hungry dream of knowledge." Like Hester's heart, Hawthorne's world is a complex "mesh of good and evil."[6]

Hawthorne's practice of fiction and James' comments on

[5] Hawthorne was aware of this problem himself, as he makes clear in the Preface to *The House of the Seven Gables*: "When romances do really teach anything, or produce any effective operation, it is usually through a far more subtle process than the ostensible one. The Author has considered it hardly worth his while, therefore, relentlessly to impale the story with its moral as with an iron rod . . ." (*The House of the Seven Gables*, Centenary Edition [Columbus: Ohio State University Press, 1965], p. 2).

[6] *Scarlet Letter*, pp. 64, 72.

it suggest the double-sided relationship between American romantics and realists. James saw himself going beyond Hawthorne, but he never rejects him. The realists could not accept romantic transcendentalism and its narrative corollaries, but they did acknowledge their debt to the romantic emphasis on personal experience, the individual, particularized description, democracy, and morality. *The Scarlet Letter* and *The Rise of Silas Lapham* are woven differently, but both concern the complex mesh of good and evil. There is no externally symbolized monkey-rope on Huck and Jim's raft, but they are as closely tied as Ishmael and Queequeg. Melville, at times, even sounds like Twain: "Better sleep with a sober cannibal than a drunken Christian."[7] *The Bostonians* rejects the emphasis on narrative incident and coincidence found in *The Blithedale Romance*, but both books explore the violation of the heart and the ambiguous relation between self-seeking and reforming.

Wordsworth's Preface to *Lyrical Ballads* can be usefully reread in the light of realistic fiction. The realists endorse Wordsworth's emphasis on "language really used by men" and "incidents and situations from common life." They too reject personifications of abstract ideas and eighteenth-century poetic diction. And the realists put the same importance on capturing experience. James, Howells, and Mark Twain each could say with Wordsworth, that "I have at all times endeavoured to look steadily at my subject."[8]

[7] Herman Melville, *Moby-Dick*, ed. Charles Feidelson, Jr. (Indianapolis: Bobbs-Merrill Co., 1964), p. 51.

[8] Preface to the second edition (1800) of *Lyrical Ballads*, *The Poetical Works of Wordsworth*, ed. T. Hutchinson and E. De Selincourt (London: Oxford University Press, 1950), pp. 734, 736. If Arthur O. Lovejoy's concepts of organicism, dynamism, and diversitarianism are accepted as romantic characteristics—opposed to neoclassic mechanism, staticism, and uniformitarianism—it is clear that realism is in some ways a continuation and development of the romantic impulse. See Lovejoy's "The Meaning of Romanticism for the Historian of Ideas," *Journal of the History of Ideas*, II (June 1941), 257–278; and *The Great Chain of Being* (New York: Harper & Row, 1960; orig. pub. 1936), esp. pp. 288–314.

Realism's dualistic relationship to pre-Civil War romantic fiction is balanced by its ambivalent relation to works written in the late 1860's and the 1870's. Local color writing is often described as "fundamentally realistic,"[9] but the fundamentals need to be clarified. The local color emphasis on ordinary people in particularized regional settings relates closely to the practice of Howells, James, and Twain in the 1880's, but not the local colorists' tendency to exaggerate and exploit the idiosyncrasies of character, dialect, and environment.

Bret Harte's cardboard characters, implausible incidents, and sentimental overwash show the wide gulf between the romances of Roaring Camp, Poker Flat, and Red Gulch and the realism of Charles Street, St. Petersburg, and Nankeen Square.[10] Edward Eggleston gave Harte credit as a "forerunner" but claimed his own *Hoosier School-Master* (1871) was the "file-leader": "For some years after [1871], my own stories had to themselves the field of provincial realism."[11] *The Hoosier School-Master*, however, is more provincial than realistic. Eggleston is an omniscient author-narrator who comments editorially on the speech and the souls of his characters. The superimposed happy ending is a good measure of his distance from the realistic fiction of the mid-1880's: "[She] fell down, faint and weary, at her blind mother's feet, and laid her tired head in her mother's

[9] Carlos Baker, "Delineation of Life and Character," *Literary History of the United States: History*, ed. R. E. Spiller *et al.*, 3d ed., rev. (New York: Macmillan Co., 1963), p. 861.

[10] Mark Twain suggests Harte's sentimentality is insincere as well as overdone. "[His] pathetics, imitated from Dickens, used to be a godsend to the farmers of two hemispheres on account of the freshets of tears they compelled. He once said to me with a cynical chuckle that he thought he had mastered the art of pumping up the tear of sensibility" (*The Autobiography of Mark Twain*, ed. Charles Neider [New York: Harper & Row, 1959], p. 137).

[11] Preface to the Library Edition of *The Hoosier School-Master* (1892); reprinted in *Selected American Prose, 1841–1900*, ed. Wallace Stegner (New York: Holt, Rinehart & Winston, 1958), pp. 310–311.

lap and wept, and wept like a child, and said, 'O mother! I'm free, I'm free!' while the mother's tears baptized her face, and the mother's trembling fingers combed out her tresses."[12] Eggleston also added a baggage-car chapter entitled "How It Came Out," which follows the characters through twenty years of ever-after happiness: "We are all children in reading stories. We want more than all else to know how it all came out at the end, and, if our taste is not perverted, we like it to come out well" (p. 174).

Edward Eggleston is not "an effectual force in the development of realistic fiction . . . striving for photographic truth in every picture,"[13] but he does move closer to realism than Bret Harte and other exploiters of the sentimental and the comic. Like the best of the regional writers (Jewett, Freeman, J. C. Harris), Eggleston favors ordinary characters —farmers, school teachers, and circuit riders—over Harte's flamboyant drunks, gamblers, and prostitutes. He also indicates an awareness of a new sensibility:

You expect me to describe that walk. You have had enough of the Jack Meanses and the Squire Hawkinses, and the Pete Joneses, and the rest. You wish me to tell you now of this true-hearted girl and her lover; of how the silvery moonbeams come down in a shower—to use Whittier's favorite metaphor—through the maple boughs, flecking the frozen ground with light and shadow. You would have me tell of the evening star, not yet gone down, which shed its benediction on them. But I shall do no such thing. For the moon was not shining, neither did the stars give their light.[14]

In spite of this romantic disclaimer (a commonplace in post–Civil War fiction), the amphibian nature of Eggleston's practice can be seen in the stultifying romance and sentiment with which he does, finally, describe that walk. Four pages later, "the moon was shining now."

[12] *The Hoosier School-Master* (New York: Hill & Wang, 1957; orig. pub. 1871), p. 169.

[13] Vernon Loggins, Introduction, *ibid.*, pp. v, ix.

[14] *Hoosier School-Master*, p. 36.

The name of John W. De Forest inevitably arises in discussions of the development of American realism. According to the *Literary History of the United States*, De Forest is "the first American writer to deserve the name of realist."[15] It is more accurate to see De Forest as a transitional author. In *Miss Ravenel's Conversion from Secession to Loyalty* De Forest uses both realistic and nonrealistic techniques. He can employ a casually omniscient style full of authorial asides, Thackerayan chapter titles, wide-ranging literary allusions, and miscellaneous commentary on his puppets—the true-blue hero, the lovely and virtuous blonde, the dark, designing woman with "beautiful, dangerous eyes," and a mustachioed villain. Yet De Forest often drops his leisurely comedy of manners to present sharp and vivid scenic portrayals of the dusty horrors of the battlefield.

The same dualism can be seen in De Forest's use of dialogue. In a relatively quiet moment the author confesses that "when I introduce a 'By Jove!' into Van Zandt's conversation, it is to be understood that that very remarkably profane officer and gentleman used the great Name of the True Divinity."[16] Twenty-five pages later a rebel soldier spots Union Captain Colburne and says, in the pleasantly murderous tone of combat, "Halt, you son of a bitch!"

Something of a realistic relativism also deepens De Forest's view of his characters. The hero is a shining knight-errant of the North, but he is naïve and stiffly idealistic, and learns to his sorrow that the wrongheaded and uneducated Southerners can be brutally tough and unflinchingly brave under fire. Carter, the villain, has all the identifying characteristics of the nineteenth-century stage landlord—mustache, alcoholism, sexual infidelity, and profanity. Yet he is a courageous man, a loyal friend, and an inspiring battle-field commander, with a surprising streak of tenderness.

[15] Gordon S. Haight, "Realism Defined: William Dean Howells," *Literary History of the U. S.: History*, p. 881.

[16] *Miss Ravenel's Conversion from Secession to Loyalty*, ed. Gordon S. Haight (New York: Holt, Rinehart & Winston, 1955), p. 268.

Miss Ravenel herself suggests some familiar stereotypes—first as pure American maiden, then as nineteenth-century Madonna. Yet Lillie is a creature of flesh and blood who steps off her pedestal to be capable of passion and sexual desire. Uninterested in matters of doctrine and ideology, she is converted from secession to loyalty through masculinity.

The war is also seen in a complex way. The North is right, yet it is prudish, stiff-necked, moralistic, and narrowminded. The South is wrong, yet like literature's greatest wrong character, Falstaff, it can be warm and witty and convivial. Northern politicians have the best cause, but Northern political corruption is dramatically portrayed in the coward Gazaway. Demon Rum is evil, but it is the teetotalers who are made to look foolish at Carter's champagne picnic. The humorously ignorant Negroes on Ravenel's plantation steal from their neighbors; and their leader, "Major" Scott, has a good deal of trouble "in regard to the Seventh Commandment." But Scott sacrifices his life for his new Union masters, and De Forest quietly notes that the defense of Fort Winthrop was greatly assisted by the Negroes, "all of whom had fought." They are a clear and effective contrast to the fort's commander, Union Major Gazaway, who fights the battle from underneath his bed.

The Civil War itself is presented by De Forest as a complex mixture of patriotic gore and glory. As they march away in chapter 8, Colonel Carter and Captain Colburne dazzle Lillie with their rich blue uniforms, brass buttons, and jaunty sabres. The regiment has a "magnificent appearance." Four hundred pages later Carter lies dead along the banks of the Cane River and Colburne returns "feeble, his eyes underscored with lines of blueish yellow, his face sallow. . . . His blouse was threadbare where the sword-belt went, and had a ragged bullet-hole through the collar."[17] The reader of *Miss Ravenel's Conversion* can only be disappointed with the saccharine domestic conclusion entitled

[17] *Ibid.*, pp. 441–442.

"A Marriage"—a hearts-and-flowers denouement which illustrates the limitation of De Forest's realistic vision.

The literary careers of the realists after the decade of the 1880's veered off in new directions. *A Hazard of New Fortunes* (1890) reflected Howells' move from Boston to New York and his deepening concern for social and economic inequities. Henry James, stunned by the lack of public success of *The Bostonians* and *The Princess Casamassima* ("They have reduced the desire, and the demand, for my productions to zero"[18]), turned to the stage and to tales which dramatized the problems of the artist. Mark Twain was forced to return to the lecture circuit in 1895, and his writings became increasingly despondent and fragmentary.

The 1890's produced a new generation of American writers and a new literary sensibility. The works of the so-called naturalists—Garland, Crane, Norris, and later, Dreiser—are often equated with those of the realists or seen as extensions of realism. This grouping is misleading; the polymorphous naturalists simultaneously accepted and rejected realism, just as the realists embraced some aspects of romanticism and repudiated others. Every literary reaction seems to incorporate part of the movement against which it is reacting. Literary history is usually a question of fathers and sons.[19]

[18] *The Notebooks of Henry James*, ed. F. O. Matthiessen and Kenneth B. Murdock (New York: Oxford University Press, 1947), p. 69.

[19] This idea is supported in an interesting way by the relation of the American realists to the French symbolists, and later, the imagists. These groups are commonly seen as a reaction to realism, yet they found their premises in the realists' redefinition of literary symbolism: "Whereas the traditional symbolist had abstracted objects into ideas, the self-proclaimed *symboliste*—as Jean Moréas announced in his manifesto of 1886—sought to invest the idea in concrete form. Hence his emphasis was on the object itself rather than its conceivable signification, on the denseness of the imagery. . . . The symbol was never clearly acknowledged [by the French symbolists] as the key to any higher plane of existence" (Harry Levin, "Symbolism and Fiction," *Contexts of Criticism* [New York: Atheneum, 1963], p. 200).

Hamlin Garland is a revealing case. A self-professed follower of Howells, Garland meant his "veritism" to be a restatement and a continuation of realism. Garland did emphasize average characters in ordinary situations, but *Main-Travelled Roads* (1891) led sharply away from the highways of the 1880's. The stories are told by an omniscient author-narrator who editorializes on tobacco chewing ("one of [Ed's] most noticeable bad habits") and the problems of city dwellers far removed from middle-border settings and unknown to his characters ("She did not know that the struggle for a place to stand on this planet was eating the heart and soul out of men and women in the city, just as in the country").[20]

The characters who trudge the main-traveled roads are painted in blacks and whites. Will Hannan has "frank, clear eyes," a "sunny smile," and a "strong brown hand." His rival, Ed Kinney, "lounged along in a sort of hang-dog style, in greasy overalls and vest unbuttoned." Ed not only chews tobacco; he trades horses (on Sunday), humiliates his wife, and berates his parents. Their conflict, in "A Branch-Road," is dissolved in a stream of pure romance—the miraculous escape from slow gray death on the farm to a life of art and leisure illuminated by the sun shining on the Bay of Naples.

Many of Garland's characters assume allegorical or epic significance. The figure of Private Smith, a returning Civil War veteran, "looms vast, his personal peculiarities fade away, he rises into a magnificent type." His return will "always remain as something epic."[21] The main-traveled road, Garland proclaimed in his epigraph, is not only in the West —it is "everywhere." It is "the main-travelled road of life."

The sterner naturalists took the low road rather than the main-traveled road. Norris and Crane turned away from realistic subject matter, moving from the average to the

[20] *Main-Travelled Roads*, ed. Thomas A. Bledsoe (New York: Holt, Rinehart & Winston, 1954; orig. pub. 1891), pp. 3, 92.
[21] "The Return of a Private," pp. 148, 152. The story ends with a projection of the next thirty years in the life of Private Smith.

subaverage. Surely Maggie's suicide, McTeague's murder of Trina, and his own Gothic doom—handcuffed without water to the body of his dead enemy in the heart of Death Valley—reflect little of the realistic concern with common, representative experience. The naturalists accept (or partially accept) a secular transcendentalism which worships at the altar of mysterious forces—environment, heredity, circumstance, chance—largely outside human control. These deterministic forces shape a fiction which frequently achieves its power through simplicity rather than through the complex density of realism. Character is de-emphasized, thus lessening the importance of individual responsibility and morality. And the naturalists, like many romantic writers, lean toward omniscient narration, reliance on incident, character types, and generalizing symbolism. What is McTeague, asks Norris, what is man, but a "half-dead canary chittering feebly in its little gilt prison?"[22]

Looking beyond the 1890's, it is clear that realism has left an important legacy to modern literature. The balance of the realists' philosophical *via media*, their subject matter, and their morality have often been neglected or transmuted in twentieth-century writing. What have not been lost, however, are the narrative developments and innovations made

[22] Frank Norris, *McTeague: A Story of San Francisco*, ed. Carvel Collins (New York: Holt, Rinehart & Winston, 1950), p. 324. Generalizations about the American naturalists are hazardous since their fiction diverged at times from their theories and the theories themselves were continually in flux. Crane is especially complex. He dramatizes the indifference of the universe and the trap of circumstance in *The Red Badge of Courage* ("He was in a moving box"), "The Blue Hotel" (men are like lice clinging to a "whirling, fire-smote, ice-locked, disease-stricken, space-lost bulb"), and "The Open Boat" (nature was "indifferent, flatly indifferent"); yet each work balances the scale through human qualities. Henry Fleming matures: "He was a man." The Easterner recognizes that "We are all in it." The survivors in the ten-foot dinghy establish a "subtle brotherhood of men . . . on the seas"(*Stephen Crane: The Red Badge of Courage and Other Writings*, ed. Richard Chase [Boston: Houghton Mifflin Co., 1960], pp. 133, 273, 309, 230, 278, 295).

by the realists—the architectural improvements in the house of fiction. It is the realistic style which has been the most influential aspect of realism for modern authors: the advances made in point of view, structural integrity, complexity of situation and character, and integrated imagery. This is what Percy Lubbock meant, when, in *The Craft of Fiction*, he stated that with James "the range of method is permanently enlarged; it is proved, once for all, that the craft of fiction has larger resources than might have been suspected before."[23] It is what Hemingway meant when he said that "all modern American literature comes from one book by Mark Twain called *Huckleberry Finn*."[24] It is what Faulkner meant when he called Mark Twain the father of Sherwood Anderson, and thus the grandfather of "my generation of American writers and the tradition of American writing which our successors will carry on."[25] Huck's particular line of succession is impressively long—George Willard, Nick Adams, Jimmy Herf, Eugene Gant, Chick Mallison, Holden Caulfield, Scout Finch—and it furnishes convincing evidence of the influence of the realists upon twentieth-century fiction.

Surely Alfred Kazin was wrong, in *On Native Grounds*, when he referred to the late nineteenth century as a "period of dark ignorance and repressive Victorian gentility" and stated that "all the birds began to sing" about 1915. What Kazin and other critics have failed to realize is that many of the songs that the birds were beginning to sing in 1915 were originally composed in 1885.

[23] New York: Viking Press, 1957 (orig. pub. 1921), p. 172.
[24] *Green Hills of Africa* (New York: Charles Scribner's Sons, 1935), p. 22.
[25] *Paris Review*, XII (Spring 1956), 46.

BIBLIOGRAPHY
AND
INDEX

HENRY JAMES

"Ivan Turgénieff." *Atlantic Monthly*, LIII (January 1884),
42–55.

"Matthew Arnold." *English Illustrated Magazine*, I (January
1884), 241–246.

"A Study of Salvini." *Pall Mall Gazette*, 27 March 1884, pp.
1–2; *Pall Mall Budget*, XXXI (28 March 1884), 9–10.
Signed "By a Casual Critic."

"Lady Barberina." *Century Magazine*, XXVIII (May–July
1884), 18–31, 222–234, 336–350.

"The Author of *Beltraffio*." *English Illustrated Magazine*, I
(June–July 1884), 563–573, 628–639.

"Pandora." New York *Sun*, 1 and 8 June 1884.

"Georgina's Reasons." New York *Sun*, 20 and 27 July, 3
August 1884.

"A New England Winter." *Century Magazine*, XXVIII
(August–September 1884), 573–587, 733–743.

"The Art of Fiction." *Longman's Magazine*, IV (September
1884), 502–521.

"The Path of Duty." *English Illustrated Magazine*, II (December 1884), 240–256.

A Little Tour in France. Boston: James R. Osgood and Co.,
1884. Originally appeared under the title *En Province* in
the *Atlantic Monthly*, vols. LII (July–November 1883) and
LIII (February, April–May 1884).

The Bostonians. Century Magazine, vols. XXIX (February–
April 1885), XXX (May–October 1885), XXXI (November–
December 1885; January–February 1886).

"George Eliot's Life." *Atlantic Monthly*, LV (May 1885),
668–678.

The Princess Casamassima. Atlantic Monthly, vols. LVI
(September–December 1885), LVII (January–June 1886),
LVIII (July–October 1886).

"Edwin A. Abbey." *Harper's Weekly*, XXX (4 December 1886), 786–787.

"William Dean Howells." *Harper's Weekly*, XXX (19 June 1886), 394–395.

"Lady Barberina" and "A New England Winter" were collected by James in *Tales of Three Cities* in 1884 (together with "The Impressions of a Cousin," originally published in *Century Magazine* in 1883). "The Author of *Beltraffio*," "Pandora," "Georgina's Reasons," and "The Path of Duty" were published in 1885 in both an American collection (*The Author of "Beltraffio"* [Boston: James R. Osgood & Co.]) and a more comprehensive English collection (*Stories Revived* [3 vols.; London: Macmillan & Co.]).

The first book publication of *The Bostonians* was the Macmillan London edition, published in February, 1886. The second edition, released three months later, was divided between the English and the American markets. Two editions of *The Princess Casamassima* were published in London by Macmillan in October, 1886, for both the domestic market and for export to America.

There are two essential bibliographical descriptions of James' writings:

Le Roy Phillips. *A Bibliography of the Writings of Henry James*, rev. ed. New York: Coward-McCann, 1930.

Leon Edel and Dan H. Laurence. *A Bibliography of Henry James*, 2d ed., rev. London: Rupert Hart-Davis, 1961.

MARK TWAIN

Adventures of Huckleberry Finn (*Tom Sawyer's Comrade*). New York: Charles L. Webster & Co., 1885. The London edition by Chatto & Windus, entitled *The Adventures of Huckleberry Finn* (*Tom Sawyer's Comrade*), was published in December, 1884, in order to establish English copyright by prior publication. The Montreal (Dawson) edition was also published in December, 1884, and the Leipzig (Tauchnitz) edition followed in January, 1885. Three selections from *Adventures of Huckleberry Finn* were printed in the

Century Magazine in 1884 and 1885, prior to the appearance of the American edition: "An Adventure of Huckleberry Finn: With an Account of the Famous Grangerford-
Shepherdson Feud" (December 1884, pp. 268–278); "Jim's
Investments, and King Sollermun" (January 1885, pp. 456–
458); "Royalty on the Mississippi: As Chronicled by
Huckleberry Finn" (February 1885, pp. 544–567).

"Mark Twain's Sketches of Henry Ward Beecher" (pp. i–iv)
and "Mark Twain's Remarkable Gold Mines" (pp. 6–7).
*Phunny Phellows: Mark Twain, Josh Billings, Robt. Bur-
dette, Artemus Ward, and Others*. Chicago: Rhodes &
McClure, 1885.

Col. Sellers as a Scientist: A Comedy [written with W. D.
Howells]. N.p., n.d. [1885?]. A two-sheet synopsis printed
for copyright purposes.

"The Private History of a Campaign That Failed." *Century
Magazine*, XXXI (December 1885), 193–204.

Mark Twain's Speeches, ed. A. B. Paine with an "Appreciation" by W. D. Howells. New York: Harper & Bros., 1923.
This volume prints eight speeches delivered by Twain
from 1884 to 1886: "Speech" ("at the Banquet of the International Congress of Wheelmen"); "Turncoats" (attacking Republicans who supported the Republican candidate, James G. Blaine, for the presidency in 1884; Twain
was a vociferous "Mugwump"); "A Tribute" (an ironic
tribute to partisanship, defeated, according to Twain, by
Grover Cleveland); "Consistency" (a defense of change
and inconsistency, with special reference to the Republicans who defected to help elect Cleveland); "Henry M.
Stanley" (Twain introduced Stanley at a Boston gathering
in November, 1886); "On Stanley and Livingstone"
(speech made in response to a toast in London's Mitre
Tavern); "General Grant's Grammar" (an attack on Matthew Arnold's criticism of Grant's *Memoirs*, published by
Twain's firm, Charles L. Webster & Co.); "The Old-
Fashioned Printer" (reminiscences about Twain's early
days as printer's apprentice).

Mark Twain: Life as I Find It, ed. Charles Neider. Garden
City, N.Y.: Hanover House, 1961. In this collection of
essays, tales, and sketches, the majority of which are

printed for the first time in book form, Neider includes four selections from the period 1884–1886: "Ah, Sin, The Heathen Chinee" (a curtain speech by Twain after a production of the play of the same name written by Twain and Bret Harte); "On Training Children" (a letter to the *Christian Union*); "Remarkable Gold Mines" (some tall tales of gold mining in the vein of *Roughing It*); "International Copyright" (Twain defends international copyright by attacking the flood of foreign literary imports, especially romances).

There is no complete bibliography of Twain's works and information about his shorter writings is particularly haphazard. The necessary beginnings to bibliographical study can be made in the following volumes, which are primarily concerned with book publication:

Jacob Blanck. *Bibliography of American Literature.* Vol. II. New Haven: Yale University Press, 1957.

Merle Johnson. *Bibliography of the Works of Mark Twain, Samuel Langhorne Clemens*, rev. and enl. New York: Harper & Bros., 1935.

WILLIAM DEAN HOWELLS

A Little Girl among the Old Masters. Boston: James R. Osgood & Co., 1884 [actually published 15 November 1883]. Introduction and comment by Howells.

"Two Notable Novels." *Century Magazine*, XXVIII (August 1884), 632–634. Reviews of *Miss Ludington's Sister* and *The Story of a Country Town.*

The Rise of Silas Lapham. Century Magazine, vols. XXIX (November 1884–April 1885), XXX (May–August 1885). The novel was published in book form by Ticknor & Co., in Boston, in August, 1885. An earlier book edition was prepared for copyright purposes by David Douglas in Edinburgh.

"The Elevator (A Farce)." *Harper's Monthly*, LXX (December 1884), 111–125.

" 'Anachronism.' " *Century Magazine*, XXIX (January 1885), 477.

"A Florentine Mosaic." *Century Magazine*, XXIX (February, April 1885), 483–501, 803–819; XXX (June 1885), 199–219.

Indian Summer. *Harper's Monthly*, vols. LXXI (July–November 1885), LXXII (December 1885–February 1886). Published in book form by Ticknor & Co., Boston, 1886. As with *Lapham*, there is an earlier Edinburgh edition (Douglas) printed for copyright purposes.

"Panforte di Siena." *Century Magazine*, XXX (August, September 1885), 534–549, 659–673.

"*Silas Lapham* and the Jews." *American Hebrew*, XXIV (4 September 1885), 50–51.

"Tuscan Cities." *Century Magazine*, XXX (October 1885), 890–910.

"The Laureate of Death." *Atlantic Monthly*, LVI (September 1885), 311–322. Concerns Italian poet Giacomo Leopardi.

"The Garroters (A Farce)." *Harper's Monthly*, LXXII (December 1885), 146–162.

Col. Sellers as a Scientist: A Comedy. N.p., n.d. [1885?]. A two-sheet synopsis written with Mark Twain and printed for copyright purposes.

"Christmas Every Day." *Saint Nicholas*, XIII (January 1886), 163–167.

The Minister's Charge; or, The Apprenticeship of Lemuel Barker. *Century Magazine*, XXXI (February–April 1886), XXXII (May–October 1886), XXXIII (November–December 1886). Published in book form by Ticknor & Co., Boston, 1887. The Edinburgh Edition (Douglas) is dated 1886.

"International Copyright." *Century Magazine*, XXXI (February 1886), 630.

"Howells' Meeting Miss Murfree." *Literary News*, VII (April 1886), 122. Excerpt from an interview. First printed in the Chicago *News*.

"Nassau," "New York Letter." *Literary World*, XVII (17 April 1886), 135. Interview.

George Fuller, His Life and Works. Boston: Houghton, Mifflin & Co., 1886.

"Mr. Howells' Work." *Literary News*, VII (May 1886), 155. Interview.

151

"New York Letter." *Literary World*, XVII (1 May 1886), 152. Speech.

"To Millicent, from America" [by Frederick Wedmore]. *Temple Bar*, LXXVII (June 1886), 241. Interview.

"The Mouse-Trap, a Farce." *Harper's Monthly*, LXXIV (December 1886), 64–75.

Not included in this bibliography are questionable attributions, earlier works reprinted from 1884 to 1886, or Howells' twelve "Editor's Study" contributions to *Harper's Monthly* (January to December, 1886), which total sixty-eight pages and include seventy-six book reviews.

The definitive bibliography of Howells' writings is *A Bibliography of William Dean Howells*, by William M. Gibson and George Arms (New York: The New York Public Library, 1948). Howells is also included in Jacob Blanck's *Bibliography of American Literature* (IV [1963], 384–448), but Blanck is heavily indebted to the Gibson and Arms volume.

Åhnebrink, Lars. "The American Scene: Social, Philosophical, and Literary Background" (pp. 1–20); "Aspects of European Realistic and Naturalistic Literature in America Prior to 1900" (pp. 34–49); "Realism in the Middle West" (pp. 50–59); "Literary Credos" (pp. 125–165). *The Beginnings of Naturalism in American Fiction: A Study of the Works of Hamlin Garland, Stephen Crane, and Frank Norris with Special Reference to Some European Influences, 1891–1903*. Upsala University Essays and Studies on American Language and Literature, vol. IX. Cambridge, Mass.: Harvard University Press, 1950. Reissued New York: Russell & Russell, 1961.

Allott, Miriam, ed. *Novelists on the Novel*, pp. 59–84. New York: Columbia University Press, 1959.

American Literary Realism: 1870–1910. Published by the University of Texas at Arlington, this new journal emphasizes the "compilation and publication of comprehensive annotated bibliographies of secondary comment on those literary figures of the designated period who have not received adequate coverage elsewhere." The Summer 1968 issue (no. 3) contains a summary of the December, 1967, Modern Language Association Conference concerning the validity and meaning of the term "realism" (pp. 73–74).

Barr, Amelia E. "The Modern Novel." *North American Review*, CLIX (November 1894), 592–600.

Becker, George J. *Documents of Modern Literary Realism*. Princeton, N.J.: Princeton University Press, 1963.

——. "Realism: An Essay in Definition." *Modern Language Quarterly*, X (June 1949), 184–197.

B[ecker], G[eorge] J., and M[onroe] C. B[eardsley]. "Realism." *Dictionary of World Literature*, rev. ed., ed. Joseph T. Shipley, pp. 335–336. Paterson, N.J.: Littlefield, Adams & Co., 1960.

Belcher, Hannah Graham. "Howells's Opinions on the Religious Conflicts of His Age As Exhibited in Magazine Articles." *American Literature*, XV (November 1943), 262–278. Reprinted in *Howells: A Century of Criticism*, ed. K. E. Eble, pp. 203–218, under the name of Graham Belcher Blackstock.

Benson, A. C. "Realism in Fiction." *Cornhill*, CV (May 1912), 605–617.

Berthoff, Warner. *The Ferment of Realism: American Literature, 1884–1919.* New York: Free Press, 1965. See especially pp. 1–47.

Besant, Walter. *The Art of Fiction.* London: Chatto & Windus, 1884. Orig. a lecture entitled "Fiction as a Fine Art," delivered at the Royal Institute in London, 25 April 1884. The essay was again reprinted in 1885, together with James' reply from the September, 1884, issue of *Longman's Magazine.* Reprinted in *Realism and Romanticism in Fiction,* ed. E. Current-García and W. R. Patrick, pp.68–85.

Blackmur, Richard P. Introduction. *The Art of the Novel: Critical Prefaces by Henry James,* pp. vii–xxxix. New York: Charles Scribner's Sons, 1934. Reprinted in the Scribner Library paperbound series, n.d.

Blair, Walter. "Literary Comedians (1855–1900)" (pp. 102–124); "The Local Colorists (1868–1900)" (pp. 124–147); "Mark Twain" (pp. 147–162). *Native American Humor.* San Francisco: Chandler Publishing Co., 1960. Orig. pub. 1937 as *Native American Humor (1800–1900).*

———. "Roots of American Realism." *University Review,* VI (June 1940), 275–281.

Blankenship, Russell. "The Rise of Realism." *American Literature As an Expression of the National Mind,* rev. ed., pp. 477–508. New York: Henry Holt & Co., 1949. Orig. pub. 1931.

Booth, Wayne C. *The Rhetoric of Fiction.* Chicago: University of Chicago Press, 1961.

Bourget, Paul. "The Limits of Realism in Fiction." *Littell's Living Age,* CXCVI (18 March 1893), 739–741.

Bowron, Bernard R., Jr. "Realism in America." *Comparative Literature,* III (Summer 1951), 268–285.

Boyesen, Hjalmar Hjorth. "The Great Realists and the Empty Story-Tellers." *Forum,* XVIII (February 1895), 724–731. Reprinted in *Realism and Romanticism in Fiction,* ed. E. Current-García and W. R. Patrick, pp. 161–168.

——. "The Progressive Realism of American Fiction." *Literary and Social Silhouettes*, pp. 58–78. New York: Harper & Bros., 1894.

——. "The Realism of the American Fiction." *Independent*, XLIV (3 November 1892), 1543–1544.

Bridgman, Richard. "Henry James and Mark Twain." *The Colloquial Style in America*, pp. 78–130. New York: Oxford University Press, 1966.

Brooks, Van Wyck. "Howells and James." *New England: Indian Summer, 1865–1915*, pp. 224–249. New York: E. P. Dutton & Co., 1940. Dutton Paperback, 1965.

——. "New York in the Eighties." *The Confident Years: 1885–1915*, pp. 1–20. New York: E. P. Dutton & Co., 1952.

Brown, Clarence Arthur. "Realism and Aestheticism." *The Achievement of American Criticism: Representative Selections from Three Hundred Years of American Criticism*, pp. 371–407. New York: Ronald Press Co., 1954.

Budd, Louis J. "W. D. Howells' Defense of the Romance." *PMLA*, LXVII (March 1952), 32–42.

Burroughs, John. "The True Realism." *Indoor Studies*, pp. 231–236. Boston: Houghton, Mifflin Co., 1889.

Cady, Edwin H. " 'Banging the Babes of Romance About' " (pp. 1–27); "The Realism War" (pp. 28–55). *The Realist at War: The Mature Years, 1885–1920, of William Dean Howells*. Syracuse: Syracuse University Press, 1958.

——. "The Editor of the *Atlantic Monthly*: 1871–1881" (pp. 157–198); "The Chief American Realist: 1881–1885" (pp. 199–245). *The Road to Realism: The Early Years, 1837–1885, of William Dean Howells*. Syracuse: Syracuse University Press, 1956.

——. Introduction. *The Rise of Silas Lapham*, pp. v–xviii. Boston: Houghton Mifflin Co., 1957.

——. "A Note on Howells and 'The Smiling Aspects of Life.' " *American Literature*, XVII (May 1945), 175–178. Reprinted in *Howells: A Century of Criticism*, ed. K. E. Eble, pp. 159–162.

——, and David L. Frazier. *The War of the Critics over William Dean Howells*. Evanston, Ill.: Row, Peterson & Co., 1962.

Caine, Hall. "The New Watchwords of Fiction." *Contemporary Review* (London), LVII (April 1890), 479–488.

Carter, Everett. "The Meaning of, and in, Realism." *Antioch Review*, XII (March 1952), 78–94.

———. "The Palpitating Divan." *College English*, XI (May 1950), 423–428. Reprinted in *Howells: A Century of Criticism*, ed. K. E. Eble, pp. 163–172, and *The War of the Critics over William Dean Howells*, ed. E. H. Cady and D. L. Frazier, pp. 194–199.

———. "Towards a Philosophy of Literary Realism" (pp. 88–169); "Critical Realism" (pp. 170–224). *Howells and the Age of Realism*. Philadelphia: J. B. Lippincott Co., 1954. Reprinted in 1966 by Archon Books, Hamden, Conn.

———. "William Dean Howells' Theory of Critical Realism." *ELH: A Journal of English Literary History*, XVI (June 1949), 151–166.

Chase, Richard. "The Broken Circuit." *The American Novel and Its Tradition*, pp. 1–28. Garden City, N.Y.: Doubleday & Co., 1957. See also Chase's note on "Norris and Naturalism," pp. 185–186, in which he distinguishes between realism and naturalism.

Clark, Kate Upson. "Realism and Romanticism." *Independent*, LII (26 July 1900), 1792–1793.

Clemens, Samuel L. *The Autobiography of Mark Twain*, ed. Charles Neider. New York: Harper & Bros., 1959. Harper & Row Perennial Classic paperback ed., n.d.

———. "Fenimore Cooper's Literary Offenses." *North American Review*, CLXI (July 1895), 1–12. See next entry.

———. "Fenimore Cooper's Further Literary Offenses," ed. Bernard De Voto. *New England Quarterly*, XIX (September 1946), 291–301. A continuation discovered by De Voto in the Mark Twain Papers. Reprinted, with the original *North American Review* article, in *The Shock of Recognition*, ed. Edmund Wilson, 1955 ed., pp. 582–594i. The "Further Offenses" are also reprinted in *Letters from the Earth*, ed. Bernard De Voto, pp. 137–145.

———. "How to Tell a Story." *Youth's Companion*, LXIX (3 October 1895), 464. Reprinted in *The Writings of Mark Twain* (New York: Harper & Bros., 1929), XXIV, 263–270.

——. *Letters from the Earth*, ed. Bernard De Voto. New York: Harper & Row, 1962.

——. "William Dean Howells." *Harper's Monthly Magazine*, CXIII (July 1906), 221–225. Reprinted in *Howells: A Century of Criticism*, ed. K. E. Eble, pp. 78–87; and partially reprinted in *The War of the Critics over William Dean Howells*, ed. E. H. Cady and D. L. Frazier, pp. 104–106.

Cunliffe, Marcus. "Realism in American Prose: From Howells to Dreiser." *The Literature of the United States*, rev. ed., pp. 185–212. Baltimore: Penguin Books, 1961. Orig. pub. 1954.

Current-García, Eugene, and Walton R. Patrick. Introduction (pp. 3–37); "Realism and Romanticism: The Critical Controversy" (selections from 13 past and present critics, pp. 40–189). *Realism and Romanticism in Fiction: An Approach to the Novel*. Chicago: Scott, Foresman & Co., 1962.

Daggett, R. M. "Motion and Emotion in Fiction: The Real versus the Realist." *Overland Monthly*, XXVI (December 1895), 614–617.

Darrow, Clarence S. "Realism in Literature and Art." *Arena*, IX (December 1893), 98–113.

Davidson, James. "John William De Forest and His Contemporaries: The Birth of American Realism." Diss., New York University, 1958.

[De Forest, John William.] "The Great American Novel." *Nation*, VI (9 January 1868), 27–29.

Duffey, Bernard I. "Hamlin Garland's 'Decline' from Realism." *American Literature*, XXV (March 1953), 69–74. See also James D. Koerner's "Comment" and Professor Duffey's "Mr. Koerner's Reply Considered," *American Literature*, XXVI (November 1954), 427–432, 432–435.

Eble, Kenneth E. *Howells: A Century of Criticism*. Dallas: Southern Methodist University Press, 1962.

Edel, Leon. "The Art of the Novel: 1884–1885" (pp. 79–146); "A London Life: 1885–1887" (pp. 147–192). *Henry James: The Middle Years (1882–1895)*. Philadelphia: J. B. Lippincott Co., 1962. Vol. 3 of Edel's biography of James.

Edgar, Pelham. "American Realism, Sex, and Theodore Dreiser." *The Art of the Novel: From 1700 to the Present Time*, pp. 244–254. New York: Russell & Russell, 1965. Orig. pub. 1933.

Edmonds, W. S. "Realism and the Real." *Dial*, XIV (16 March 1893), 173–174.

Edwards, Herbert. "Howells and the Controversy over Realism in American Fiction." *American Literature*, III (November 1931), 237–248. Reprinted in *Howells: A Century of Criticism*, ed. K. E. Eble, pp. 119–131.

Eggleston, Edward. Preface. *The Hoosier School-Master*. Library Edition, 1892. Reprinted in *Selected American Prose*, ed. Wallace Stegner, pp. 310–323.

Ellmann, Richard, and Charles Feidelson, Jr. "Realism." *The Modern Tradition: Backgrounds of Modern Literature*, pp. 229–378. New York: Oxford University Press, 1965.

Falk, Robert P. "The Literary Criticism of the Genteel Decades, 1870–1900." *The Development of American Literary Criticism*, ed. Floyd Stovall, pp. 113–157. Chapel Hill, N.C.: University of North Carolina Press, 1955. Paperbound reprint by the College & University Press of New Haven, Conn., 1964.

——. "The Rise of Realism, 1871–1891." *Transitions in American Literary History*, ed. H. H. Clark, pp. 381–442. Durham, N.C.: Duke University Press, 1953.

——. "The Search for Reality: Writers and Their Literature." *The Gilded Age: A Reappraisal*, ed. H. W. Morgan, pp. 196–220. Syracuse: Syracuse University Press, 1963.

——. *The Victorian Mode in American Fiction, 1865–1885*. East Lansing, Mich.: Michigan State University Press, 1964.

Firkins, O. W. "The Irresponsible Power of Realism." *North American Review*, CCXXIII (March–April–May 1926), 131–144.

Flanagan, John T. "Joseph Kirkland, Pioneer Realist." *American Literature*, XI (November 1939), 273–284.

Forster, E. M. *Aspects of the Novel*. New York: Harcourt, Brace & Co., 1927. Reprinted 1954.

Fox, Arnold B. "Howells' Doctrine of Complicity." *Modern*

Language Quarterly, XIII (March 1952), 56–60. Reprinted in *Howells: A Century of Criticism*, ed. K. E. Eble, pp. 196–202.

Friedman, Norman. "Point of View in Fiction: The Development of a Critical Concept." *PMLA*, LXX (December 1955), 1160–1184.

Gale, Zona. "Period Realism." *Yale Review*, XXIII (Autumn 1933), 111–124.

Garland, Hamlin. *Crumbling Idols: Twelve Essays on Art Dealing Chiefly with Literature, Painting, and the Drama.* Chicago: Stone & Kimball, 1894. John Harvard Library Paperback, ed. Jane Johnson, 1966.

————. "Mr. Howells's Latest Novels." *New England Magazine*, II (May 1890), 243–250. Partially reprinted in *Howells: A Century of Criticism*, ed. K. E. Eble, pp. 54–59; and in *The War of the Critics over William Dean Howells*, ed. E. H. Cady and D. L. Frazier, pp. 48–50.

Gerber, John C. "The Relation between Point of View and Style in the Works of Mark Twain." *Style in Prose Fiction: English Institute Essays, 1958,* ed. Harold C. Martin, pp. 142–171. New York: Columbia University Press, 1959.

Gohdes, Clarence. "Realism for the Middle Class." *The Literature of the American People: An Historical and Critical Survey,* ed. A. H. Quinn, pp. 661–680. New York: Appleton-Century-Crofts, 1951.

Gore, Luther Y. " 'Literary Realism or Nominalism' by Ellen Glasgow: An Unpublished Essay." *American Literature*, XXXIV (March 1962), 72–79.

Gorlier, Claudio. "William Dean Howells e le definizioni del realismo." *Studi americani*, II (1956), 83–125.

Gosse, Edmund. "The Limits of Realism in Fiction." *Forum*, IX (June 1890), 391–400. Reprinted in *Realism and Romanticism in Fiction*, ed. E. Current-García and W. R. Patrick, pp. 140–148.

Haight, Gordon S. Introduction. *Miss Ravenel's Conversion from Secession to Loyalty,* pp. v–xx. New York: Holt, Rinehart & Winston, 1955.

————. "Realism Defined: William Dean Howells." *Literary History of the United States: History,* ed. R. E. Spiller *et al.*

3d ed., rev., pp. 878–898. New York: Macmillan Co., 1963. Orig. pub. 1948.

Hale, E. E. "Some Further Aspects of Realism." *Dial*, XIV (16 March 1893), 169–171.

Hamilton, Clayton. "Romance and Realism." *Dial*, XXXVII (16 November 1904), 295–297.

Hart, James D. "Realism." *The Oxford Companion to American Literature*, 4th ed., p. 698. New York: Oxford University Press, 1965.

Hatcher, Harlan. "The Rise of Realism." *Creating the Modern American Novel*, pp. 3–106. New York: Farrar & Rinehart, 1935. Reissued New York: Russell & Russell, 1962.

Hazlitt, Henry. "Realism versus Romance." *The Anatomy of Criticism*, pp. 233–269. New York: Simon & Schuster, 1933.

Hoffman, Daniel G. "Retrospect: Reality as Fable." *Form and Fable in American Fiction*, pp. 353–359. New York: Oxford University Press, 1961.

Hoffman, Frederick J. "Henry James, W. D. Howells, and the Art of Fiction." *The Modern Novel in America*, rev. ed., pp. 1–30. Chicago: Henry Regnery Co., 1963. Orig. pub. 1951.

Horton, Rod W., and Herbert W. Edwards. *Backgrounds of American Literary Thought*, pp. 122–250. New York: Appleton-Century-Crofts, 1952.

Howard, Leon. "The Search for Reality." *Literature and the American Tradition*, pp. 199–230. Garden City, N.Y.: Doubleday & Co., 1960.

Howells, Mildred, ed. *Life in Letters of William Dean Howells*. 2 vols. Garden City, N.Y.: Doubleday, Doran & Co., 1928.

Howells, William Dean. "Editor's Study." *Harper's Magazine*, January 1886 to March 1892. Edited and rearranged (with omissions) as *Criticism and Fiction* (New York: Harper & Bros., 1891). Reprinted several times during Howells' lifetime and recently in *Criticism and Fiction and Other Essays*, ed. Clara M. and Rudolf Kirk (New York: New York University Press, 1959).

——. "Henry James, Jr." *Century Magazine*, XXV (November 1882), 25–29. Reprinted in *William Dean Howells: Representative Selections*, ed. Clara and Rudolf Kirk, pp. 345–355.

——. *Literary Friends and Acquaintance: A Personal Retrospect of American Authorship*. New York: Harper & Bros., 1900.

——. *Literature and Life: Studies*. New York: Harper & Bros., 1902.

——. *My Literary Passions*. New York: Harper & Bros., 1895.

——. *My Mark Twain: Reminiscences and Criticisms*. New York: Harper & Bros., 1910. Partially reprinted in *The Shock of Recognition*, ed. Edmund Wilson, pp. 674–741.

Hubbell, Jay B. "The Rise of Realism, 1870–1914." *American Life in Literature*, rev. ed., II, 1–20. New York: Harper & Bros., 1949. Orig. pub. 1936.

James, Henry. "The Art of Fiction." *Longman's Magazine*, IV (September 1884), 502–521. James' reply to Walter Besant's essay of the same title, reprinted in 1885 (with Besant's article) and collected by James in *Partial Portraits* in 1888.

——. *The Art of the Novel: Critical Prefaces by Henry James*, ed. Richard P. Blackmur. New York: Charles Scribner's Sons, 1934. Reprinted in the Scribner Library paperbound series, n.d.

——. *Essays in London and Elsewhere*. London: James R. Osgood, 1893.

——. *French Poets and Novelists*. London: Macmillan & Co., 1878.

——. *The Future of the Novel: Essays on the Art of Fiction*, ed. Leon Edel. New York: Vintage, 1956.

——. "The Great Form." *Literary Opinion in America*, ed. M. D. Zabel, I, 56–57. A letter orig. pub. in the New York *Tribune*, 4 August 1889, and reprinted by Leon Edel in the London *Times Literary Supplement*, 29 July 1939, p. 460.

——. *Hawthorne*. London: Macmillan & Co., 1879. Written for the English Men of Letters Series, ed. John Morley. Reprinted in *The Shock of Recognition*, ed. Edmund Wilson, pp. 427–565.

——. *The Notebooks of Henry James,* ed. F. O. Matthiessen and Kenneth B. Murdock. New York: Oxford University Press, 1947. Galaxy Book, 1961.

——. *Notes and Reviews.* Cambridge, Mass.: Dunster House Press, 1921.

——. *Notes on Novelists; With Some Other Notes.* New York: Charles Scribner's Sons, 1914.

——. *Partial Portraits.* London and New York: Macmillan & Co., 1888.

——. *Views and Reviews.* Boston: Ball Publishing Co., 1908.

——. "William Dean Howells." *Harper's Weekly,* XXX (19 June 1886), 394–395. Reprinted in *The Shock of Recognition,* ed. Edmund Wilson, pp. 570–579; and in *Howells; A Century of Criticism,* ed. K. E. Eble, pp. 41–50. Partially reprinted in *The War of the Critics over William Dean Howells,* ed. E. H. Cady and D. L. Frazier, pp. 42–45.

Jones, Arthur E., Jr. "Darwinism and Its Relationship to Realism and Naturalism in American Fiction, 1860 to 1900." *Drew University Bulletin,* XXXVIII (December 1950), 3–21.

Jones, Howard Mumford. " 'A Usable Past.' " *The Theory of American Literature,* pp. 118–159. Ithaca, N.Y.: Cornell University Press, 1965. Reissue, with a new concluding chapter and revised bibliography. Orig. pub. 1948.

Kaul, A. N. "Concluding Note: Social Reality and the Form of American Fiction." *The American Vision: Actual and Ideal Society in Nineteenth-Century Fiction,* pp. 305–323. New Haven, Conn.: Yale University Press, 1963.

Kazin, Alfred. "The Opening Struggle for Realism." *On Native Grounds: An Interpretation of Modern American Prose Literature,* pp. 3–50. New York: Harcourt, Brace & Co., 1942. Doubleday Anchor Book ed., abridged with a Postscript, 1956.

Kirk, Clara M. "Reality and Actuality in the March Family Narratives of W. D. Howells." *PMLA,* LXXIV (March 1959), 137–152.

Kirkland, Joseph. "Realism versus Other Isms." *Dial,* XIV (16 February 1893), 99–101.

Knight, Grant C. "The Literature of Realism." *American Literature and Culture*, pp. 331–497, esp. pp. 358–388. New York: Ray Long & Richard R. Smith, 1932.

Lease, Benjamin. "Realism and Joseph Kirkland's *Zury*." *American Literature*, XXIII (January 1952), 464–466.

Lebowitz, Martin. "Concerning Realism in Literature." *Journal of Philosophy*, XXXIX (18 June 1942), 356–359.

Leisy, Ernest Erwin. "The Advance of Realism in Howells and James." *American Literature: An Interpretative Survey*, pp. 187–200. New York: Thomas Y. Crowell Co., 1929.

Levin, Harry. "The Context of Realism" (pp. 64–73); "The Dynasty of Realism" (pp. 74–83). *The Gates of Horn: A Study of Five French Realists*. New York: Oxford University Press, 1963.

——. "Symbolism and Fiction." *Contexts of Criticism*, pp. 190–207. Cambridge, Mass.: Harvard University Press, 1957. Atheneum ed., 1963. Originally presented in 1956 to the Peters Rushton Seminar on Contemporary Prose and Poetry and published by the University of Virginia Press.

——. "What Is Realism?" *Comparative Literature*, III (Summer 1951), 193–199. Originally delivered before the Comparative Literature section of the Modern Language Association, 30 December 1948. Reprinted in *Contexts of Criticism*, Harvard University Press, 1957, pp. 67–75.

Levy, Leo B. "Naturalism in the Making: De Forest's *Honest John Vane*." *New England Quarterly*, XXXVII (March 1964), 89–98.

Light, James F. *John William De Forest*. New York: Twayne Publishers, 1965.

Liljegren, Sten B. *The Revolt against Romanticism in American Literature As Evidenced in the Works of S. L. Clemens*. Upsala University Essays and Studies on American Language and Literature, vol. I, 1945. Reissued New York: Haskell House, 1964.

Linneman, William R. "Satires of American Realism, 1880–1900." *American Literature*, XXXIV (March 1962), 80–93.

Lubbock, Percy. *The Craft of Fiction*. New York: Charles Scribner's Sons, 1921. Viking Press Compass Books ed., 1957.

Mabie, Hamilton Wright. *Books and Culture.* New York: Dodd, Mead & Co., 1896.

——. "The Two Eternal Types in Fiction." *Forum,* XIX (March 1895), 41–47.

——. "A Typical Novel." *Andover Review: A Religious and Theological Monthly,* IV (November 1885), 417–429. Partially reprinted in *The War of the Critics over William Dean Howells,* ed. E. H. Cady and D. L. Frazier, pp. 38–41. Review of *The Rise of Silas Lapham.*

McIntyre, Clara F. "J. W. De Forest, Pioneer Realist." *University of Wyoming Publications,* IX (31 August 1942), 1–13.

McMahon, Helen. *Criticism of Fiction: A Study of Trends in the "Atlantic Monthly," 1857–1898.* New York: Record Press, 1952.

McMurray, William. *The Literary Realism of William Dean Howells.* Carbondale, Ill.: Southern Illinois University Press, 1967.

——. "Pragmatic Realism in *The Bostonians.*" *Nineteenth-Century Fiction,* XVI (March 1962), 339–344.

Magnus, Julian. "A Plea for Reality in Plays." *Century Magazine,* XXXI (November 1885), 155–156.

Mallock, W[illiam] H. "The Relation of Art to Truth." *Forum,* IX (March 1890), 36–46. Reprinted in *Realism and Romanticism in Fiction,* ed. E. Current-García and W. R. Patrick, pp. 129–138.

Malone, Clifton. "The Realism of William Dean Howells." *Quarterly Bulletin of Oklahoma Baptist University (Faculty Studies, No. 2),* XXXIV (February 1949), 3–22.

Mariani, Umberto. "Il realismo di John W. De Forest." *Studi americani,* VII (1961), 77–103.

Martin, Harold C. "The Development of Style in Nineteenth-Century American Fiction." *Style in Prose Fiction: English Institute Essays, 1958,* pp. 114–141. New York: Columbia University Press, 1959.

Martin, Jay. *Harvests of Change: American Literature, 1865–1914.* Englewood Cliffs, N.J.: Prentice-Hall, 1967.

Marx, Leo. "The Pilot and the Passenger: Landscape Conventions and the Style of *Huckleberry Finn*." *American Literature*, XXVIII (May 1956), 129–146.

Matthews, Brander. "Mr. Howells as a Critic." *Forum*, XXXII (January 1902), 629–638. Reprinted in *Howells: A Century of Criticism*, ed. K. E. Eble, pp. 65–77; and *The War of the Critics over William Dean Howells*, ed. E. H. Cady and D. L. Frazier, pp. 83–90.

Maxwell, D. E. S. "Edith Wharton and the Realists" (pp. 236–264); "Appendix B" (pp. 294–299). *American Fiction: The Intellectual Background*. New York: Columbia University Press, 1963.

Meserve, Walter J. "Truth, Morality, and Swedenborg in Howells' Theory of Realism." *New England Quarterly*, XXVII (June 1954), 252–257.

Mizener, Arthur. "The American Novel and Nature in the Nineteenth Century" (pp. 105–118); "The Realistic Novel as Symbol" (pp. 267–287). *The Sense of Life in the Modern Novel*. Boston: Houghton Mifflin Co., 1964.

Morgan, H. Wayne, ed. *The Gilded Age: A Reappraisal*. Syracuse: Syracuse University Press, 1963. Syracuse University Paperback ed., 1964.

Muller, Herbert J. "Realism." *Modern Fiction: A Study of Values*, pp. 37–49. New York: Funk & Wagnalls Co., 1937. McGraw-Hill paperback ed., 1964.

Nelson, John Herbert, and Oscar Cargill. "Contemporary Trends." *Contemporary Trends: American Literature since 1900*, rev. ed., pp. 1–25. New York: Macmillan Co., 1949. Orig. pub. 1933.

"The New School of American Fiction." *Temple Bar* (London), LXX (March 1884), 383–389.

Norris, Frank. *The Responsibilities of the Novelist and Other Literary Essays*. New York: Doubleday, Page & Co., 1903.

Ohmann, Richard M. "Prolegomena to the Analysis of Prose Style." *Style in Prose Fiction: English Institute Essays, 1958*, pp. 1–24. New York: Columbia University Press, 1959.

Paine, Albert Bigelow. *Mark Twain: A Biography; The Personal and Literary Life of Samuel Langhorne Clemens*. 3 vols. New York: Harper & Bros., 1912.

Parrington, Vernon L. "The Development of Realism." *The Reinterpretation of American Literature*, ed. Norman Foerster, pp. 139–159. New York: Russell & Russell, 1959. Orig. pub. 1928.

——. "Victorian Realism." *The Beginnings of Critical Realism in America: 1860–1920* (vol. III of *Main Currents in American Thought*), pp. 237–253. New York: Harcourt, Brace & Co., 1930. Harbinger Book, 1956.

Pattee, Fred Lewis. *A History of American Literature since 1870*. New York: Century Co., 1915.

Peckham, H. Houston. "Lopsided Realism." *South Atlantic Quarterly*, XV (July 1916), 276–281.

Pellew, George. "The New Battle of the Books." *Forum*, V (July 1888), 564–573. Reprinted in *Realism and Romanticism in Fiction*, ed. E. Current-García and W. R. Patrick, pp. 120–128.

Perry, Bliss. "Realism." *A Study of Prose Fiction*, pp. 217–257. Boston: Houghton Mifflin Co., 1902. Rev. ed., 1920.

Perry, T[homas] S[ergeant]. "Mark Twain." *Century Magazine*, XXX (May 1885), 171–172. Review of *Adventures of Huckleberry Finn*.

Picht, Douglas R. "William Dean Howells: Realistic-Realist." *Research Studies*, XXXV (March 1967), 92–94.

Pizer, Donald. *Realism and Naturalism in Nineteenth-Century American Literature*. Carbondale, Ill.: Southern Illinois University Press, 1966.

Poirier, Richard. *A World Elsewhere: The Place of Style in American Literature*. New York: Oxford University Press, 1966.

Porter, Charlotte. "The Serial Story." *Century Magazine*, XXX (September 1885), 812–813.

Price, Robert. "Mrs. Catherwood's Early Experiments with Critical Realism." *American Literature*, XVII (May 1945), 140–151.

Pritchard, John Paul. "The Realists." *Criticism in America*, pp. 163–190. Norman, Okla.: University of Oklahoma Press, 1956.

Quinn, Arthur Hobson. "The Transition to Realism" (pp.

159–204); "William Dean Howells and the Establishment of Realism" (pp. 257–278); "The Development of Realism" (pp. 433–471). *American Fiction: An Historical and Critical Survey*. New York: D. Appleton-Century Co., 1936.

———. "William Dean Howells and the Approach to Realism" (I, 66–81); "James A. Herne and the Realism of Character" (I, 125–162); "William Gillette and the Realism of Action" (I, 212–238); "The New Realism of Character" (II, 207–239). *A History of the American Drama From the Civil War to the Present Day*, rev. ed., 2 vols. in 1. New York: Appleton-Century-Crofts, 1943.

Rahv, Philip. "Paleface and Redskin" (pp. 1–6); "The Cult of Experience in American Writing" (pp. 7–25). *Image and Idea*, rev. and enl. ed. New York: New Directions, 1957. "The Cult of Experience" orig. pub. in *Partisan Review*, VII (November–December 1940), 412–424.

Ransom, Ellene. *Utopus Discovers America; or, Critical Realism in American Utopian Fiction, 1798–1900*. Nashville: Joint University Libraries, 1947.

Ratner, Marc L. "Howells and Boyesen: Two Views of Realism." *New England Quarterly*, XXXV (September 1962), 376–390.

Richardson, Charles F. "Later Movements in American Fiction." *American Literature: 1607–1885*, II, 413–450. New York: G. P. Putnam's Sons, 1888.

———. "The Moral Purpose of the Later American Novel." *Andover Review*, III (April 1885), 312–325.

Roberts, Robert R. "Gilt, Gingerbread, and Realism: The Public and Its Taste." *The Gilded Age: A Reappraisal*, ed. H. W. Morgan, pp. 169–195. Syracuse: Syracuse University Press, 1963.

Rubin, Louis D., Jr., and John Rees Moore, eds. *The Idea of an American Novel*, pp. 61–87. New York: Thomas Y. Crowell Co., 1961.

Salomon, Roger B. "Realism as Disinheritance: Twain, Howells and James." *American Quarterly*, XVI (Winter 1964), 531–544.

Saum, Lewis O. "The Success Theme in Great Plains Realism." *American Quarterly*, XVIII (Winter 1966), 579–598.

Scholes, Robert, ed. *Approaches to the Novel: Materials for a Poetics,* rev. ed., pp. 43–136. San Francisco: Chandler Publishing Co., 1966. Orig. pub. 1961.

——, and Robert Kellogg. *The Nature of Narrative.* New York: Oxford University Press, 1966. Galaxy paperbound ed., 1968.

Smith, Bernard. "Democracy and Realism." *Forces in American Criticism: A Study in the History of American Literary Thought,* pp. 134–184. New York: Harcourt, Brace & Co., 1939.

Smith, Henry Nash, and William M. Gibson, eds. *Mark Twain–Howells Letters: The Correspondence of Samuel L. Clemens and William D. Howells, 1872–1910.* 2 vols. Cambridge, Mass.: Harvard University Press, 1960.

Smith, Lewis Worthington. "The Drift toward Naturalism." *South Atlantic Quarterly,* XXII (October 1923), 355–369.

Snell, George D. "Realists." *The Shapers of American Fiction, 1798–1947,* 2d ed., pp. 198–300. New York: Cooper Square, 1961. Orig. pub. 1947.

Spencer, Benjamin T. "The Impulse to Realism" (pp. 134–139); "The Ascendance of Indigenous Realism" (pp. 319–328). *The Quest for Nationality: An American Literary Campaign.* Syracuse: Syracuse University Press, 1957.

——. "The New Realism and a National Literature." *PMLA,* LVI (December 1941), 1116–1132.

Spiller, Robert E. "Father of Modern American Realism." *Saturday Review,* XXXIII (2 September 1950), 10–11.

——. "Literary Rediscovery: Howells, Mark Twain." *The Cycle of American Literature: An Essay in Historical Criticism,* pp. 141–162. New York: Macmillan Co., 1955. Mentor Book ed., 1957.

Stallman, Robert Wooster, ed. *The Critic's Notebook,* pp. 39–56. Minneapolis: University of Minnesota Press, 1950.

Stanley, Hiram M. "The Passion for Realism, and What Is to Come of It." *Dial,* XIV (16 April 1893), 238–240.

Stegner, Wallace. Introduction. *Selected American Prose: 1841–1900,* pp. v–xxvi. New York: Holt, Rinehart & Winston, 1958.

Stevenson, Robert Louis. "A Humble Remonstrance." *Longman's Magazine*, V (November 1884), 139–147. Reprinted in *Realism and Romanticism in Fiction*, ed. E. Current-García and W. R. Patrick, pp. 110–118. Stevenson's contribution to the Besant-James debate.

Stone, Albert E., Jr. "Reading, Writing, and History: Best Novel of the Civil War." *American Heritage*, XIII (June 1962), 84–88.

Strauss, Harold. "Realism in the Proletarian Novel." *Yale Review*, XXVIII (Winter 1939), 360–374.

Stromberg, Roland N., ed. *Realism, Naturalism, and Symbolism: Modes of Thought and Expression in Europe, 1848–1914*. New York: Harper & Row, 1968.

Stronks, James B. "William Dean Howells, Ed Howe, and *The Story of a Country Town*." *American Literature*, XXIX (January 1958), 473–478. Reprinted in *Howells: A Century of Criticism*, ed. K. E. Eble, pp. 152–158.

Sullivan, Philip Edward. "John William De Forest: A Study of Realism and Romance in Selected Works." Diss., University of Southern California, 1966.

Taylor, Houghton W. "Some Nineteenth Century Critics of Realism." *University of Texas Studies in English*, No. 8 (8 July 1928), pp. 110–128.

Taylor, Walter Fuller. "The Changing Age and the Realistic Impulse" (pp. 219–231); "Emerging Types of Realism" (pp. 261–279). *The Story of American Letters*, rev. ed. Chicago: Henry Regnery Co., 1956. Orig. pub. 1936.

Thayer, William R. "The New Story-Tellers and the Doom of Realism." *Forum*, XVIII (December 1894), 470–480. Reprinted in *Realism and Romanticism in Fiction*, ed. E. Current-García and W. R. Patrick, pp. 150–159; and partially reprinted in *The War of the Critics over William Dean Howells*, ed. E. H. Cady and D. L. Frazier, pp. 67–71.

Thompson, Maurice. "The Domain of Romance." *Forum*, VIII (November 1889), 326–336.

Thorp, Willard. Introduction. *Great Short Works of American Realism*, pp. xiii–xxii. New York: Harper & Row, 1968.

Thrall, William F., and Addison Hibbard. "Realism" (pp. 397–399); "Realistic Period in American Literature, 1865–1900" (pp. 400–402). *A Handbook to Literature*, rev. and enl. by C. Hugh Holman. New York: Odyssey Press, 1960. Orig. pub. 1936.

Trilling, Lionel. "Manners, Morals, and the Novel." *Kenyon Review*, X (Winter 1948), 11–27. Reprinted in *The Liberal Imagination* (New York: Viking Press, 1950), pp. 205–222.

——. "Reality in America." *The Liberal Imagination*, pp. 3–21. New York: Viking Press, 1950. Part i orig. pub. in *Partisan Review*, VII (January–February 1940), 24–40; part ii orig. pub. in *Nation*, CLXII (20 April 1946), 466–472.

——. "W. D. Howells and the Roots of Modern Taste." *Partisan Review*, XVIII (September–October 1951), 516–536. Reprinted in *The Opposing Self: Nine Essays in Criticism* (New York: Viking Press, 1955), pp. 76–103; and partially reprinted in *The War of the Critics over William Dean Howells*, ed. E. H. Cady and D. L. Frazier, pp. 208–220.

Van Doren, Carl. "Howells and Realism." *The American Novel, 1789–1939*, rev. and enl. ed., pp. 115–136. New York: Macmillan Co., 1940. Orig. pub. 1921.

——. "The Later Novel: Howells." *The Cambridge History of American Literature*, III, 66–95. New York: Macmillan Co., 1933. Orig. pub. 1917.

Vogelback, Arthur Lawrence. "The Publication and Reception of *Huckleberry Finn* in America." *American Literature*, XI (November 1939), 260–272.

Wagenknecht, Edward. "The Realistic Ideal." *Cavalcade of the American Novel*, pp. 130–135. New York: Henry Holt & Co., 1952.

Walcutt, Charles Child. *American Literary Naturalism: A Divided Stream*. Minneapolis, Minn.: University of Minnesota Press, 1956.

——. "Frank Norris on Realism and Naturalism." *American Literature*, XIII (March 1941), 61–63.

Wann, Louis. "The Rise of Realism." *The Rise of Realism: American Literature from 1860 to 1900*, rev. ed. (vol. III of

American Literature: A Period Anthology, ed. Oscar Cargill), pp. 1–22. New York: Macmillan Co., 1949. Orig. pub. 1933.

Warfel, Harry R. "The Author's Neutrality in Realistic Fiction." *Florida Quarterly*, I (Summer 1967), 23–29.

Warner, Charles Dudley. "Modern Fiction." *Atlantic Monthly*, LI (April 1883), 464–474. Reprinted in *Realism and Romanticism in Fiction*, ed. E. Current-García and W. R. Patrick, pp. 54–66.

Watson, H. B. Marriott. "The Old Controversy." *Living Age*, CCXXXIX (14 November 1903), 430–439.

Watt, Ian. "Realism and the Novel Form" (pp. 9–34); "Realism and the Later Tradition: A Note" (pp. 290–301). *The Rise of the Novel: Studies in Defoe, Richardson and Fielding*. Berkeley, Calif.: University of California Press, 1957.

Weinberg, Bernard. "Conclusions." *French Realism: The Critical Reaction, 1830–1870*, pp. 192–199. New York: Modern Language Association of America, 1937. See also pp. 126–127 for a formulation of realistic theory in French fiction.

Wellek, René. "The Concept of Realism in Literary Scholarship." *Concepts of Criticism*, ed. Stephen G. Nichols, Jr., pp. 222–255. New Haven, Conn.: Yale University Press, 1963.

——. "Henry James's Literary Theory and Criticism." *American Literature*, XXX (November 1958), 293–321.

——, and Austin Warren. "The Nature and Modes of Narrative Fiction." *Theory of Literature*, 3d ed., pp. 212–225. New York: Harcourt, Brace & World, [1963].

Westbrook, Max. "The Critical Implications of Howells' Realism." *Texas Studies in English*, XXXVI (1957), 71–79.

Williams, Raymond. "Realism and the Contemporary Novel." *Partisan Review*, XXVI (Spring 1959), 200–213.

Wilson, Edmund. "The Chastening of American Prose Style; John W. De Forest." *Patriotic Gore: Studies in the Literature of the American Civil War*, pp. 635–742. New York: Oxford University Press, 1962.

——, ed. *The Shock of Recognition: The Development of Literature in the United States Recorded by the Men Who*

Made It. Garden City, N.Y.: Doubleday, Doran & Co., 1943. Grosset's Universal Library ed., 1955.

Wright, Walter F. "The Ultimate Theme: The Quest for Reality." *The Madness of Art: A Study of Henry James*, pp. 155–209. Lincoln: University of Nebraska Press, 1962.

Zabel, Morton Dauwen. "Introduction: Criticism in America." *Literary Opinion in America*, 3d ed., rev., I, 1–43. New York: Harper & Row, 1962. Orig. pub. 1937.

Ziff, Larzer. *The American 1890's: Life and Times of a Lost Generation.* New York: Viking Press, 1966.

Zola, Émile. "The Experimental Novel" (pp. 1–54); "The Novel: The Reality" (pp. 209–223); "The Novel: Morality" (pp. 282–287). *The Experimental Novel and Other Essays*, trans. Belle M. Sherman. New York: Haskell House, 1964. Orig. pub. 1893. *Le Roman expérimental* was first published in Paris in 1880.

The Illusion of Life
was composed and printed by
    Heritage Printers, Inc.,
    Charlotte, North Carolina.
It was bound by
    Carolina Ruling and Binding Co., Inc.,
    Charlotte, North Carolina.
The paper is Warren's Olde Style,
    and the type is Palatino.
Design is by Edward G. Foss.